MASTERING THE ART OF CAREER CHANGE

DESIGN YOUR FUTURE, TELL YOUR STORY, AND BUILD A CAREER YOU LOVE

JORDAN BLAKE

Copyright © 2025 BY Synast Publishing

Published by Synast Publishing

All rights reserved.

ISBN: 978-1-968418-45-8

INTRODUCTION

On a typical Monday morning, the air is thick with the sense of routine. Yet, for many, this routine is cloaked in a feeling of discontent, a silent whisper of "there must be more." This book is crafted for those who feel this tug, a guide for individuals ready to redefine their professional trajectory. It speaks directly to those feeling trapped in roles that no longer fulfill them, addressing the common fears of financial insecurity, self-doubt, and the daunting task of starting anew.

The motivation behind this book stems from a deep-seated passion for seeing professionals unlock their potential and find joy in their careers. Drawing from personal experiences and extensive research, it offers readers not just inspiration but a concrete blueprint for change. This is not about generic advice; it is about providing actionable strategies, real-life case studies, and interactive tools to navigate the complexities of career transformation.

Readers will find themselves armed with a personalized roadmap, gaining clarity and confidence as they progress. The book delves into the science of change, demystifying the psychological barriers that often hinder career shifts. It guides readers through self-assessment, helping them uncover core motivations and align their future paths with their deepest values.

Addressing skepticism head-on, the book provides real-world testimonials and data to reassure readers that they are not alone and that change is possible at any age or stage. The structure of the book is designed to lead readers through a logical progression from mindset shifts to opportunity mapping, personal branding, and ultimately, life integration.

This book is not just a read but a journey, an invitation to engage actively with its exercises and resources. It encourages readers to revisit chapters, utilize its digital companion tools, and join a supportive community. The message is clear: career change is achievable, and with the right guidance, it can lead to a fulfilling and purpose-driven professional life.

Table of Contents

Chapter 1: Facing Change: Mindset, Motivation, and Mapping Your Why

Breaking Free from Feeling Stuck

Think about how you would feel waking up every morning with a sense of dread, knowing that the day is going to be full of tasks that do not in any way stir some feeling of passion or purpose in you. This sentiment is not new to most people who feel trapped in a career and feel that it is not a way of finding fulfilment. The feeling of trappiness is not only some short period of disgruntlement, but a rather deep-rooted and permeating feeling of being stuck in some cycle that does not appear to have an escape. The accumulation of stress usually complements this emotional pit, the deterioration of mental health, and the sense of time wasted that cannot be re-obtained.

The repercussions of not acting upon this entrapment are severe. The stress level can be increased due to prolonged dissatisfaction, which has some negative effects on health and personal relationships. The longer a person stays in such a state, the deeper the feeling gets rooted, and opportunities to grow and develop are missed. It is important to note the stagnation indications and start resisting the stagnation in its face.

Making sense of why change is so difficult is one of the steps towards achieving a breakthrough. The psychological studies point out the idea of loss aversion and a habit loop as pitfalls on the way to change. There is a natural tendency of people to avoid losses instead of possible benefits, and the prospect of abandoning a familiar, even dissatisfactory, position is paralyzing. Also, the cognitive and behavioral repetition forms a comfort zone that is restricting but appears safe.

The answer to this is first to diagnose the trapped feeling candidly and honestly. This is by admitting the emotions and pinpointing the particular aspects of the present job that lead to this feeling of being confined. Is it the absence of promotion, the incongruence of values, or maybe the tediousness of the day-to-day grind? These factors are the key to liberation, and understanding them is a step in that direction.

A practical exercise may achieve this breakthrough: imagine that change is possible. The possibility of imagining some other reality, a reality in which passion and mission become the leading qualities of everyday life at work, makes it a bit easier to regard the present state not as a sentence but as a provisional one. This exercise will not only help one understand what is holding one back but also give one the bravery to see new horizons.

Finally, to overcome the feeling of being stuck, it is essential to have a paradigm shift in the approach to the profession. It is about redefining success not only in the financial accolade or position, but in self-fulfilment, development, and input. The change may be revolutionary and can be used to re-invent what might have been considered an insurmountable obstacle.

Therefore, the quest to escape is not just a matter of switching jobs; it is a matter of switching outlooks. It is about the need to embrace the discomfort of the unknown and have faith in one's own capabilities in handling the new challenges. Through knowledge of the psychological obstacles to change and by consciously, purposefully approaching them, one will be able to make the mindset of the trapped into a potent force to make a positive change.

Pinpointing Your Why

Think about how great it would be to wake up each day with a feeling of purpose and place, knowing why you are doing what you are doing. This is the ability to find your why in your career path. It is all about going down to the base of the surface desires that usually obscure our vision, such as better pay or a fancy title, to find out what we are really motivated by. It is a process that demands looking inward and being truthful, and therefore, he is urging you to look deeper and deeper and go beyond the here and now and look deeper and deeper to the deeper and enduring.

When this exploration starts, you are advised that you should reflect on your past experiences to discover the patterns of satisfaction and dissatisfaction. These trends usually tell about some undercurrents that have driven your professional satisfaction or dissatisfaction. Maybe you have realized that the jobs that provided you with freedom and autonomy in their approach, as well as the ones that offered greater creativity, have been happier than the ones that were structured and/or micromanaged. The observations are important because they assist in moulding a better image of what exactly really matters to you.

The next thing is to build a bright picture of your future career. Imagine a day within the dream work life--think about the setting, the contacts, and the emotion it produces. Is it a team room that is full of inventive activities or a secluded area where one can concentrate and make personal input? This vision is your light; it directs your choices and gives you something to compare the opportunities.

A good why is a very powerful weapon when faced with difficulties. It serves as a stabilizing agent and can work against fears of doubt and keep the momentum when losses are experienced. It is why you will stick to it when the going gets tough and will provide insight and strength.

It is not only a process of going inside to find your why, but also going outside to relate. It entails a conversation with mentors, peers, and even strangers who may also provide tips and viewpoints that you may not have thought of. Such discussions may open opportunities and ways that can support your underlying inspirations.

Finally, the aim of identifying your why is to create a successful career, one worth living with. It is about doing what you believe in and enjoy in your work, so that with every move you make, you take a step closer. It is this alignment that makes a job a calling, which gives life to your career, making it purposeful and satisfying. This way, you craft a career path that is yours and one that is supportive of your broader goals and aspirations in life.

Therefore, the search for your why is a continuous process that develops as you grow and transform. It is a promise to oneself that one does not live in mediocrity but instead dreams of a profession that satisfies their needs as well as nourishes their souls. This is what a career vision of purpose entails, a vision of promise not only of success, but of fulfillment of depth.

Naming and Taming Career Change Fears

Fear is a very stubborn force in the context of career transitions. Such fears take different shapes, which include but are not limited to financial insecurity, age concerns, the effects on the family, loss of status, and fear of failure. All of these fears, although intimidating, are common to people who consider such a great change. These fears are important issues that should be understood and addressed in order to find a way towards a new career.

One of the first items on the list of those with career changes in mind is financial fears. The future of lower-income individuals or the necessity to invest in further education may be daunting. Nevertheless, it should be noted that the aspects of financial fears, although legitimate, are manageable through proper planning. Setting a realistic budget, or even side hustling, or even a bridge job, can help them feel more financially steady in the transition period.

Another common concern is age-related fears. A lot of people fear that they are too old to begin again or that younger ones will have an advantage. Nevertheless, experience and maturity might be strong tools. Experienced career changers tend to carry a lot of experience and a developed set of skills that could be of great use in a new position. There are new opportunities that can be accessed by challenging the belief that age will be a barrier.

Another important issue is the effect of a career change on the family. The anxiety of the impact of a change in career on the family roles and responsibilities can be intimidating. The fears can be reduced by open communication with family members about the changes that may occur. It could be discussed to get the family support and understanding about the benefits of the change, like greater job satisfaction or better work-life balance.

There is also the fear of the loss of status or professional identity. Most people are scared of the fact that a transferred job may be on a lower level, or they would not be respected as they are at their present job. The way to reframe this fear is to understand the importance of beginning anew and the possibility of progress and new accomplishments. It is possible to preserve personal brand and use transferable skills to support personal identity throughout the transition.

Lastly, fear of failure is paralysing. The threat of failing in a new career may discourage most people even before they make the transition. It would be wise to note that any form of growth involves failure. Resilience and persistence can be encouraged by adopting the attitude that negative events are a part of the learning process and not a fixation on failure.

Action-oriented strategies are helpful in adequately coping with these fears. The methods that may be useful include the ability to break down fears into small, manageable components, find mentorship, and use positive self-talk. Strategies such as these may be practiced to gain confidence and alleviate the anxiety of career change.

To conclude, career change fears are not easy, but they are not impossible. By labeling those fears and taking proactive actions to improve upon them, people may turn their fear into motivation, and this is the way to a successful and full-fledged career transition. This can be a difficult trip to make, yet through proper thinking and equipment, it is possible.

Rewriting Limiting Beliefs

Below the surface of our psychology, we have limiting beliefs that tend to creep into our psyche and mold our perceptions, thus determining what we do and how we behave. These beliefs are the chains that keep us in one place and fail to achieve our full potential, and this applies in the case of changing careers. They mumble, tell stories of insufficiency, elitism, and insignificance, and cause us to question our abilities and dread the unknown. The only way to escape these mental shackles is first to unearth these submerged scripts and challenge their soundness.

The first step to transformation is to identify limiting beliefs. These assumptions tend to be deeply rooted, and they are supported by years of personal and work experiences. These are in the form of thoughts such as: I am too old to begin over, I do not have the relevant skills, or Networking is not my thing. It is essential to see such thoughts as a construction, not as a truth. This awareness opens the gateway to disrupting and ultimately rewriting these narratives.

The refutation of these beliefs needs information and practical demonstration. Take into account the number of people who have made a career change later on in life, or those who have moved into completely different areas. Their narratives are effective counter-narratives to the restrictive beliefs that imply that some paths are either not practicable or impossible. It is possible to start unraveling the lies that restrict potential by being around good examples and stories of success.

Cognitive reframing is an effective instrument of the process. It entails changing attitude and perceiving events in a more empowering way. Mere changes in attitude and journaling can do it. An example would be turning around the "I am too old" and turning it to bring a wealth of knowledge and wisdom, and this is going to make the difference. This new attitude can be solidified further through journaling that invites one to think about previous achievements and future goals.

Another effective strategy is empowering oneself with micro-wins. Smaller and attainable aims can build confidence and, in the process, deconstruct systemic beliefs. Informational interviews, participation in skill-building workshops, or even volunteering in a new area may become real evidence that a person will be able to adjust and succeed. Such minor achievements lead to the development of a feeling of ability and the willingness to take more significant challenges.

It is a very personal, transformative process in the end to rewrite limiting beliefs. It takes guts to deal with the fears and doubts that have been ingrained after a long time. However, with the challenge and redefinition of these notions, a new freedom is discovered. This is not the only freedom regarding career opportunities; all spheres of life are open to it and allow people to follow the paths according to their inner passions and values.

Rewriting limiting beliefs is not a one-day process. It requires patience, perseverance, and the desire to face unpleasant facts. Yet, the rewards are profound. Breaking these mental barriers would open up the world of possibilities, and the person would be armed with the confidence and clarity to guide them through the career transitions they have entered. This metamorphosis is not simply of occupational reiteration, but of re-creating one's story and writing his or her own destiny that is not only satisfactory but also conformist to the utmost desire. By doing so, the rework of restrictive beliefs will be a foundational pillar of personal and professional development, and a stronger and more genuine life will appear.

Chapter 2: Unpacking You: Values, Strengths, and Transferable Skills

Discovering Your Core Values

In seeking a satisfying vocation, it is most important to know what ultimately motivates you. Core values are the unspoken guide that sets the course of action, determines decisions, and makes you the kind of professional you are. They define who you are and what you represent, and they are deeply incorporated into your personal and professional life. The identification of such values is not just a self-awareness activity but a strategic weapon that may result in your greater fulfillment and a more successful career.

This self-discovery of your values starts with introspection. It takes an honest examination of what is really important to you, not the veneer of titles, wages, or even social norms. This inquiry will entail looking at moments of high and low satisfaction and discontent in your professional life. Consider how you were most energized and passionate in a way that felt authentic. On the other hand, think of those moments when you felt exhausted or those moments when you felt in conflict with your identity. Those reflections are able to demonstrate some hidden values that are either being respected or infringed upon.

Structured exercises could be of great help in enabling this discovery. Begin by making a list of words or phrases that have a deep inner feel to you. These may be concepts such as integrity, innovation, collaboration, or autonomy. After a preliminary list, now rank these values in order of the ones you will not be willing to forgo. This prioritization assists in the separation of values that are core to your identity and those that are desirable.

It is important to know what is meant by misalignment of values. The culture of your work or the environment where you work may end up being incompatible with your values, which results in dissatisfaction, stress, and feeling out of place. This can be corrected by having a nagging sensation that something is wrong, although you are not able to place your finger on exactly what that is. With time, it will wear down your motivation and affect your general well-being. By identifying such red flags in time, you can avoid the long-term frustration and pursue more consistent career opportunities.

Core values must be used to gauge career opportunities once they have been identified. In a new position or project, evaluate how the position or project fits your values. This congruence serves as a test run on the prospective satisfaction and success. As an example, when innovation is at the heart of your values, look at the environment that supports innovation and experimentation. If cooperation is also important, then focus on teams and organizations that encourage a collaborative and inclusive culture.

Furthermore, the core values do not remain constant and can change with your development and experience. Consistent reflection and re-evaluation make sure that your profession is in sync with your developing personality. This practice can be introduced into your working routine, which will help in endless development and satisfaction.

Fundamentally, learning and identifying with your values is not merely a matter of self-discovery but also designing a career that is not merely successful but highly fulfilling. This is the key to an effective career change that will lead you towards a successful career change because this is the focus on personal values and professional life that is aligned.

Uncovering Hidden Strengths

When trying to change their careers to pursue fulfilling work, people tend to forget about the internal merits that are hidden under the veil of their jobs. It starts with some basic differences between abilities and strengths. The acquired abilities, which are developed through time through practice and repetition, are skills. They consist of the practical skills that can be added to a resume. On the contrary, strengths refer to hereditary gifts that are natural and are the ones that make one vibrate and stand out. Realizing this difference is very important in the process of career change.

A process of intense introspection, and other people discover these hidden strengths. It must be a conscious endeavor to strip away the day-to-day in the busyness of activities and assignments to get to what is really driving and motivating. Practical aids that may be used during this phase of discovery are self-assessment tools, peer response, and reflective journaling. They assist in discovering those skills that cannot be observed at once but are still important in developing a new career direction.

Unorthodox or soft strengths usually emerge as the main ones in the context of career transition. Adaptability, empathy, and process improvement qualities are some of the qualities that have been invaluable in industries. These are not necessarily the strengths as outlined in the conventional job descriptions, but they are the much-needed strengths in the current dynamic work settings. Such strengths can make one stand out among others in a competitive job market as they indicate the capability to cope with change and relate with other people.

The second action to take on the strengths to capitalize on them is to fit them into the possible new roles. This is done by plotting out how these inherent attributes can be implemented in other situations, thus forming a connection between the past and the future. It is important to communicate these strengths in the interview or other networking opportunities. It involves the development of a story that will categorically explain how such strengths will make a difference in the success of a new employer or industry.

Discovering the concealed strengths is not only about figuring out how to find them and how to put them into words; it is also all about accepting them as the foundation of a professional shift. It is a change of mindset whereby the attitudes held towards these strengths are not to consider them as side effects of the previous positions in life, but see them as the sources of future success. It is about being able to realize that these strengths do not just stand firm, but they can be dynamic and change with new opportunities and challenges.

Finally, the ability to discover concealed strengths is a radical process. It gives people the strength to go beyond the boundaries of their present job descriptions and see the enormous potential that is there. It creates a spirit of confidence and openness to self-growth, making one welcome to take charge of his or her own career development. By paying more attention to such strengths that people tend to underestimate, one can design a profession that will not only fit his/her capabilities and background but also reflect his/her interests and desires. This is critical towards long-term satisfaction and success in any career change undertaking.

Mapping Transferable Skills

Maps of transferable skills and their ability to identify and chart such skills are one of the most significant aspects of the career change process. It is these skills that provide a channel through which past experiences are matched with prospects, and people can cross industries with conviction and ability. It is important to start with the definition of transferable skills: they are skills and expertise that apply to different contexts and positions and are not limited by the context of particular job titles or industries. These skills are very important to hiring managers since they show the potential of a person to change and succeed in new conditions.

Mapping these skills is initiated by a planned skill-mapping exercise. This is done by motivating people to enlist all their capabilities, classifying them according to their usability in various sectors. In so doing, it is possible to focus on skills that have cross-industry appeal, including communication, leadership, problem-solving, and adaptability. It also requires one to reflect on previous jobs and experiences in order to pinpoint areas where the skills can be tapped, regardless of the job.

In order to support this translation, it is necessary to offer templates to rewrite the skills. These templates act as a restructuring guide to re-frame skills in a manner that is acceptable to hiring managers in new areas. As an example, the skill of dealing with classroom dynamics can be converted to cross-functional team leadership in the context of project management positioning. Not only does such translation make skills relatable, but it also customizes them to the language and expectations of various industries.

Examples can be provided with specific, industry-specific examples to demonstrate such concepts with a lot of clarity. Through the mini-case studies, individuals would be able to view real-life stories of how the skills have been effectively transferred across industries. A former teacher who has moved to a training position in a corporation could point out his/her experience in curriculum development, such as creating and putting in place all-inclusive training programs. Not only does this reframing demonstrate the applicability of their experience, but it also makes it consistent with the demands of the new job.

Moreover, a skills inventory workbook can become a priceless weapon in this procedure. This workbook will make people look beyond the conventional resumes and make them add non-conventional experience like volunteering, hobbies, or duties in the military or family life. With such a thorough inventory, people can discover previously neglected skills that might not become obvious at first sight but can be very valuable in new jobs.

It is also important to note that there are bridge or hybrid skills. These are skills that incorporate aspects of several fields, such as technical skills and communication skills. Such hybrid skills are now becoming more and more sought after in the modern, changing job market, and they offer a competitive advantage to people looking to switch careers.

Finally, the necessity to offer evidence cannot be overestimated. The combination of any skill with real evidence in terms of metrics, stories, or concrete accomplishments provides credibility and richness to the skill set. This fact can reinforce the story, and at the same time, it can be used to make real examples, which can be used in interviews or in letters of application.

Overall, transferable skills mapping is a strategic process, which implies the process of recognizing, translating, and presenting your skills. It is a matter of closing the gap between previous experiences and future opportunities and making sure that people can offer themselves as flexible and worthy candidates for any job change.

The Skills Inventory Workbook

The Skills Inventory Workbook can become a crucial resource in the context of career transformation, being carefully structured so that it can help individuals to reveal and rank their long-forgotten competencies. This workbook is both a transitional tool between one's past life experience and future aspirations, in that it serves as a structured place to record skills that may not have typically been listed on a resume. It promotes holistic exploration that goes beyond the usual assignments and calls on people to explore non-standard activities like volunteering, leisure, military service, or family commitments.

The workbook focuses on finding and describing what are called bridge or hybrid skills, or skills that combine technical and interpersonal skills, which are in demand more and more in the current employment environment. The workbook makes users aware of the importance of these hybrid skills by encouraging them to acknowledge them in various industries. An example is a skill set that comprises technological skills and communication skills, which can be a big asset in a position that involves cross-functional teamwork.

The main idea of the workbook is the imposition of evidence-based skill identification. Every competence mentioned above has concrete evidence, including narrative, measurements, or outcomes, which turns the abstract into the concrete. This strategy not only enhances the personal realization of what he or she can do but also offers interesting stories that can be used in interviewing and networking.

The workbook is also used to guide the refreezing of professional experiences, especially for those who are moving to new industries. It provides narrative strategies, including the "Situation-Action-Result" (SAR) model, with the help of which one can create a story that will appeal to prospective employers. The workbook provides the ability to translate past experiences into pertinent stories, thus enabling the user to portray themselves as a diverse and flexible candidate.

Besides, the Skills Inventory Workbook is not only about enumerating skills but about identifying trends and prospects. It promotes self-reflection, which makes users recognize how their competencies can be used in new situations, which also contributes to the spirit of development and potential. This is a critical reflective practice in the process of considering a career pivot since it instills confidence and clarity in the professional identity and future direction.

The Skills Inventory Workbook, in the real sense, is not just a set of exercises, but it is a metamorphosis that helps an individual with the instruments to beat the odds that come with a career change. It is a resource that assists the path from uncertainty to empowerment and enables people to see not only their current strengths but also to see how they may be in the future, and even in new and exciting ways. The workbook offers a means through which people can define their worth in a language that appeals to the modern labor market and thus can be deemed as an invaluable addition to the arsenal of career-changing tools.

Chapter 3: Reframing Experience for New Industries

The Power of Narrative in Career Change

Storytelling as an art is also an effective instrument in the complex context of career change, and it changes the way people narrate their career paths. It is not a simple re-telling of the role history or a resume of responsibilities, but a living, breathing thing, and it can give a person breathing life into a career past and shape the skills and experiences to be viewed in a new perspective, indicating that a person is heading in a new direction later on.

The central theme of this change is the idea that facts and figures, though not unimportant, hardly reflect the spectrum of the capabilities and potential of an individual. Rather, stories provide a comprehensive perspective, a perspective that is contextually rich and emotive, and can appeal to potential employers at a more profound level. Using stories of the things that happened to anyone in the past, professionals will have an opportunity to show not only what they have performed, but also how they handled the challenges, how they coped with the hurdles, and what they have learnt in the process.

The organized narrative forms like the "Situation-Action-Result" (SAR) or "Challenge-Action-Outcome" templates give the template of how to create these narratives. The models can assist in simplifying complicated experiences to meaningful, digestible narratives that depict essential thinking, problem-solving proficiencies, and adaptability, which are so valued in any career setting. These stories will allow a career changer to turn an ordinary job into an exciting account of innovation, leadership, or perseverance.

In addition, it is important to make these narratives specific to the audience. The story could be overstated or understated in a resume, during an interview, or at a networking event. Every platform gives a different chance to emphasize various features of the story, so that the message reaches the target audience. For example, a story about team leadership may be more appropriate for an interview, and a story about technical competencies may be more appropriate for a resume.

Another strength of narrative is that it is effective in overcoming the imposter syndrome that most people often face during career changes. Categorizing their experiences as narratives of their development and success, people will be able to strengthen their belief in being competent and willing to take new challenges. This redefining assists in the acknowledgment and expression of one's self-worth in a novel environment, transforming self-doubt into self-confidence.

Storytelling is also important to practice. To create a narrative is not sufficient, but one should perfect it with feedback and improvement. The exercises that include telling the stories to peers or mentors may be extremely instructive and allow refining the narrative to make it both meaningful and genuine. This is not only practical in making the story better, but also the speaker of the story is able to deliver it with a belief and certainty.

Finally, the story is a transitional one, one that connects the dots of the past and the possible. It is an instrument that, when used well, could turn what would otherwise be a career change into a journey. Learning how to tell a story, people are able to deal with the intricacies of career change with confidence, clarity, and meaning, and make their stories not only heard but remembered.

Structured Storytelling Frameworks

Just picture one being at the edge of the new career and wonder at the possibilities available, but it seems overwhelming. Storytelling becomes your map, and it leads you to the unexplored land of career change. The core of this strategy is a developed storytelling structure, a device that moves beyond narration and is a connective point between experiences of the past and future dreams.

Structured storytelling is not merely about narrating the previous roles and duties; rather, it is an integrated narrative that appeals to future employers and working partners. This model focuses on the strength of the so-called Situation-Action-Result (SAR) model, which is the approach that changes ordinary job descriptions into impressive stories.

Putting the experiences into this frame, you show not only the hardships undergone but also the actions and the very real outcome of the actions. This is what impresses the listener much more, and it gives you an insight into your abilities and potential.

In a systematic form of storytelling, you are able to put your previous roles into narratives that fit the requirements of new industries. This does not only entail changing job titles or restructuring duties. It demands an in-depth knowledge of the language and values of the target industry, and this enables you to shape your story so that it appeals to a particular audience. This personalisation is important, since it shows your adaptability and your success in new settings, overcoming any doubt about your change.

Write to the audience as you develop your story. Be it the resume, interview, or a networking discussion, the story you convey should be relevant and interesting. It has to address the interests and priorities of your audience using the language and examples they will know and like. This is where the art of storytelling really serves its purpose since you are able to convey complicated ideas and experiences in a relatable and effective manner.

It is necessary to practice and polish your storytelling skills. Do practice-based exercises that allow you to rehearse and get feedback to make sure that your story is well-edited and convincing. It is an interactive process that will improve not only your storytelling skills but also instill confidence that will help you portray your career change with credibility and conviction.

In addition, one of the most effective ways to overcome imposter syndrome, which affects career changers, is through storytelling. Focusing on your accomplishments and the different viewpoint you have to offer, storytelling can be used to promote your worth and potential further, overcoming your own doubts with evidence of what you have already accomplished.

Structured storytelling is your friend in the career change journey, making the unknown opportunity. It is a tactical device that not only explains your history but also sheds light on your future, giving you a clear direction in the huge world of career options. By storytelling, you not only narrate your story but also create your career narrative, developing a future that fits your goals and abilities.

Overcoming Imposter Syndrome

One such issue permeates all aspects of career transition, and it is the overriding sense of imposture in some quarters, which is often paralysing and demoralising. This is usually referred to as imposter syndrome; this is an internalized, persistent fear of being revealed as a fraud, despite apparent success and ability. It occurs especially in people who go into new areas of professional life or abandon old jobs.

Imposter syndrome starts mostly with self-doubt, a quiet voice that believes that one is undeserving and incapable of performing well in a new career. What makes this self-doubt is a habit of downplaying accomplishments and past successes as a factor of chance or timing. People can find themselves in one of the comparison traps, where they can compare their new competencies with the experienced competencies of others, which will only contribute to their insecurities.

These thought patterns must be identified and vigorously deconstructed in order to sail across these turbulent waters. The first important step to be made is to recognize the fact that imposter syndrome is universal; people of all spheres and successes have it. It is often freeing to realize that these feelings are not special or reflective of real incompetence.

One of the best methods of overcoming imposter syndrome is to establish self-confidence in transferable skills. That includes conscious reformulation of self-doubt by concentrating on the achievements of the past and the value that the person can bring to a new position. Having a list of achievements, even very minor, and looking at it periodically can act as an effective reminder of oneself and one's own potential. Also, soliciting advice from trusted peers or mentors may be a way of outside confirmation and support self-confidence.

There can also be real-life stories of transformation that can be used as a light of hope and inspiration. Think about the story of an experienced specialist who successfully switched to a totally new sphere of activity and conquered his or her imposter complex by adhering to the specific vision and talents. Such tales create hope of development and achievement, despite self-distrust.

There are also practical exercises that can support such a path of overcoming imposter syndrome. Cognitive reframing is one exercise of identifying and challenging limiting beliefs. Written down and vigorously challenged by evidence of successful cases in the past, these beliefs can be changed over time by transforming the attitude of inadequacy to competence and potential.

To sum up, a breakthrough in career change is one of the most important processes that can be achieved by overcoming imposter syndrome. It entails a deliberate action to identify and change the negative thinking habits, the ability to appreciate one's own competencies and worth, and a willingness to self-improve. Through these practices, one is able to change self-doubt to self-assurance, and this will lead to the successful transition of their career.

Designing Your Next Chapter

To think of a new chapter in your career, it is necessary to start with an in-depth study of new areas and development segments. As the present environment is changing fast, it is imperative to rely on trusted data from the labor market to track trends and demand positions. Use such resources as the Bureau of Labor Statistics and job boards in specific industries to find information about such industries as renewable energy, cybersecurity, and healthcare technology. Such areas not only portend growth but also align with careers that are future-proofed.

After you understand what opportunities are available, conduct specific research into every industry. It includes the installation of tools such as Google Alerts, the trends in the industry, the utilization of sites such as Glassdoor to evaluate the culture of the company, and informational interviews to obtain inside opinions. This comprehensive research will contribute to finding culture fit and making sure that prospective employers have similar values and career goals.

It is essential to undertake an analysis of the gap between the skills and abilities that you have and those that you need in the new area as you plan out your next career step. This discussion will point out areas to work on and show you the way to develop the required skills in an efficient way (using online courses, workshops, or on-the-job training). Take into account whether a formal education is indispensable or if microlearning and the acquisition of specific skills can close the gap more successfully.

The idea of a bridge job may be a useful stepping stone, where you are trying new horizons with financial stability. These part-time and/or freelance positions can be invaluably informative and help you see whether the new direction is a direction you want to pursue in the long run. The stories of successful professionals who have employed bridge roles to ease their way into their preferred industries and emerge successful through competence and confidence are rampant.

Another very important thing to do when planning your career's next chapter is to plan your transition timeline. This includes developing a step-by-step approach that takes into consideration financial, family, and emotional preparedness.

Use electronic tools and templates to monitor the progress, so that your transition can be as smooth as possible. Flexibility in your plan and regular reviews will enable you to make the needed adjustments and not lose momentum.

Creation of a personal brand is part of the process. Write a powerful story that explains your career shift in a clear and easy-to-understand manner, focusing on your personal strengths and the value you will add to the new industry. Exploit social networking sites such as LinkedIn to make you more visible so that your profile includes your new career goals and is edited with the right keywords.

Lastly, use the strength of storytelling to present your career change when networking and interviewing. Write a simple and true narrative that not only elaborates your transition but also demonstrates that you are passionate and willing to take new challenges. Adapt this story to the needs of various audiences, and make sure it appeals to potential employers.

Through methodical opportunity seeking, skill gap bridging, and planning your next career transition, you can create a rewarding and successful second phase of your career. This preemptive strategy not only gets you ready to face the world that lies ahead of you but also provides you with the instruments and confidence to succeed in your new corporate life.

Chapter 4: Exploration, Research, and Opportunity Mapping

Scanning the Horizon

It takes more than a surface look at job adverts to peer into the horizon of career opportunities. It is a thorough study of the labor market to determine the sectors that are likely to grow and that are in line with the laborers' capacity-building needs. This discovery period resembles testing the tides of an expansive ocean in which the horizon is filled with new industries that carry different opportunities to those who can adjust and be creative.

It is necessary to have the updated data on labor markets to understand the dynamics of the growth sectors. The Bureau of Labor Statistics, LinkedIn Economic Graph, and similar resources can offer a lot of information on the trends in the industry, its future growth, and the positions that are in demand at the moment. Analyzing this information, it is possible to understand in which areas the expansion is observed, as well as in which skills are obsolete. This information serves as a compass, assisting people in navigating their professional directions toward fields that have the most opportunities for future-proofing their professions.

Renewable energy, cybersecurity, healthcare technology, and remote-first workforces are among the industries that have seen fast growth. Not only are these industries flourishing, but they are also transforming the manner in which we consider work. An example of this is the increasing necessity to adopt sustainable practices, which has increased the need to hire people with sustainability manager skills. In contrast, the emergence of AI created the role of an AI project coordinator. These functions are an indication of a shift in the conventional type of job (i.e., the digital age).

In this process, decoding job postings and company news becomes a very important skill. It goes beyond reading the listed requirements; it involves reading between the lines to see new trends and opportunities that may not be obvious on the surface. This skill enables job seekers to observe future needs and to present themselves as proactive job seekers who are willing to respond to future challenges.

The landscape presents customized opportunities to individuals moving out of various sectors. Education professionals, especially former educators, may have a natural shift to EdTech, and those in the financial industries may shift to fintech startups. These transitions are enabled through the recognition of bridge or hybrid skill sets that represent competencies that cut across multiple areas, e.g., technical skill sets coupled with good communication skills.

In addition, it is important to do preliminary opportunity research. This can be achieved by establishing alerts on industry trends, relying on such tools as Glassdoor and Vault to learn about companies, and participating in job boards or job newsletters specific to the industry. This kind of systematic plan is such that the decisions regarding career choices made by an individual are guided by up-to-date, comprehensive data, instead of assumptions made in the past.

Scanning the horizon, in a nutshell, is a matter of controlling one's career path. It is a well-planned venture involving the use of data-oriented information coupled with a good sense of individual strengths and market demands. In this way, they not only are ready to take the next step, but they also develop an attitude of constant learning and adjusting, which are important qualities in the modern professional environment that is constantly changing.

Industry Deep Dives

A survey of the landscapes of several industries shows a web of possibilities for career changers. This terrain is a minefield that one should navigate with a specific strategy to discover the buried treasures and possible traps in every sector. The methodical analysis of the tendencies in the industry, its development, and the number of new types of jobs is essential to those who intend to make a switch. It includes the exploitation of such resources as the Bureau of Labor Statistics and the LinkedIn Economic Graph to obtain current and up-to-date information. Job boards and industry-specific newsletters also offer great information about the new trends in the industry and the positions that are being sought.

The knowledge of the processes that spur development in specific industries could be an important element in career choice. Future-proof sectors are suggested to include industries like renewable energy, cybersecurity, healthcare technology, and remote-first workforces. The disciplines have strong prospects because they are evolving fast, and there is a need for skilled professionals in these fields. Career changers are able to identify such high-opportunity fields, and this can help them match what the market needs more closely, based on their skills and interests.

Being able to interpret job descriptions and company announcements with a sharp eye will enable people to see trends and positions that might not have been there several years ago. In such a way, new positions are developed, such as sustainability manager or AI project coordinator, as organizations respond to the new challenges and technologies. Early identification of these trends will give a competitive advantage in the employment market.

In addition, the provision of industry snapshots and identification of hot jobs that people with diverse backgrounds can be used to give a practical guide to career changers. As an example, when former teachers move to EdTech or finance professionals mid-career to fintech startups, they illustrate how transferable skills can help them get into new sectors.

Targeted opportunity research is a crucial skill that is necessary to assess particular areas and employers. This can be automated by creating a repeatable workflow, e.g., by setting up Google Alerts to keep up with industry trends and using websites like Glassdoor and Vault. Also, the measuring of culture fit and work values using company mission statements and employee reviews are additional measures of how a company or sector fits with individual priorities.

Another very important part of industry research is the preparation of informational interviews. Developing closed-ended questions and plans to have inside sources of information about the field of work and the people already working in the field stimulates the knowledge and development of valuable networks. Monitoring results with the help of digital tools, such as spreadsheets or applications, such as Notion or Trello, is a sure way to maintain structured and convenient information.

When assessing whether a field is a good fit, red flags and green flags should be assessed through the formulation of checklists. The high turnover rates may be a warning sign, but the focus on either mentorship or career development may be a positive indicator. Early detection of these signs enables career changers to make well-planned choices that are in tandem with their values and strengths.

Utilizing online forums and reviews in the form of Reddit or professional forums provides uncensored feedback and practical information. Successful and unsuccessful mini case studies of pivots explain why such evaluations are important. Career changers can make smarter choices by learning through the experience of others.

Red Flag and Green Flag Checklists

When traveling through the dense world of career change, it is important to learn to detect the nuanced clues that may signal possible obstacles or opportunities. And this is where the idea of red flags and green flags comes into play. These checklists can be used as a guideline to analyze new careers and the possibility of a new opportunity to help one identify the pattern between the career that fulfills his/her principles and the one that can cause disappointment.

Red flags are danger signs that are indicative of possible problems or a lack of focus with personal or professional aspirations. This may be in the form of high turnover rates in an organization, which may be a sign of a poisonous work environment or lack of stability. Red flags can also be viewed as a deficiency of clear advancement opportunities or the lack of mentorship programs, implying a low growth potential. Moreover, to the extent that one of the companies advertises itself as flexible and does not provide the opportunity to work remotely, it might fail to embrace the idea of work-life balance that is often a decisive feature among numerous professionals.

Green flags, on the other hand, are good signs that indicate being in tune with career goals and values in life. These may entail a high focus on mentoring and career growth, which implies an accommodating environment that attaches importance to employee development. Firms with strong training regimes and skill upgrading opportunities are also regarded as favorable ones, as they show their interest in employee development and innovation. A green flag can also be a clear company culture that matches personal values, like an aspiration to be a sustainable company or a diverse company.

It is important to identify these flags at the early stages of the career exploration process. It helps people make better choices and not waste time and effort on avenues that might not end up making them happy. Such discrimination is especially significant in a world where employment and business cultures may differ significantly from what is on the surface.

People need to complete intensive research and contemplation in order to make good use of such checklists. This can be done by researching the company reviews, interacting with the current or previous employees, and evaluating the compatibility of the company's values with personal priorities. LinkedIn, Glassdoor, and industry-specific forums can serve as a resourceful source of information about the culture of the company and employee satisfaction.

Further, the use of these checklists is not only about traps to be avoided but also about pursuing opportunities that are appealing to career objectives. Using green flags, one will be able to follow positions that will not only be aligned to their skillset but will also provide them with a satisfying job experience that will support personal and professional development.

To conclude, the red flag and green flag checklists belong to the career change toolbox. They enable people to explore the job market with confidence so that their next career move is not merely a strategic one but also fulfilling and in line with their future aspirations. Being mindful and assertive means that career changers are able to locate not only a job, but also a position that truly fits them in terms of values and aspirations and opens the door to a gratifying career path.

Conducting Gap Analyses

Within the complex process of managing career change, determining and managing gaps in skills is a critical action that may greatly influence the success of the transition. Gap analysis is a very important tool in this venture as it enables one to identify the gap between their present skills and the skills they need in their preferred jobs. This critical thinking process not only identifies areas to be improved upon but also gives an organized means of closing such gaps effectively without necessarily having to start anew in the career.

In order to start a gap analysis, we must first define the target role or industry. This clarity makes the other steps clear, so that the skills that are being determined as requirements are truly in line with the career objectives. The practical way is to break up job descriptions and expectations of the industry in order to elicit a list of specific competencies required. This list can be considered as a standard by which one can evaluate his/her current abilities.

After defining the skills needed in the new role, the next step is to do a candid self-assessment. These include mapping current skills and experiences against what has been identified. Using a structured worksheet to list these competencies is advantageous, as it is possible to have a graphic illustration of the presence of the gaps. This practice not only provides clarity, but it is also beneficial in determining which capabilities require instant focus.

The strategies needed to fill these gaps may not necessarily involve any formal schooling. More often than not, strategic learning and development can be realized in a more adaptable and expedient way. Coursera or LinkedIn Learning are online platforms that offer more specific courses that can be completed at one's own pace and thereby have the chance of learning new skills within a short time. In addition, pursuing stretch assignments in the present job may provide some on-the-job experience that supplements learning.

Another effective way of acquiring skills can be volunteering to work on projects within and outside an organization when one is already employed. Such opportunities not only offer real-world experience but also increase the professional network, which can be beneficial during a career. Moreover, microlearning, or learning in little, concentrated pieces, may serve as an efficient method of skill acquisition in bits.

Another crucial question to be answered is whether or not it is necessary to go back to formal education. In the case of others, further certification and a degree may be justified, particularly when credentialing is strongly emphasized in the target industry. Nonetheless, a decision tree method can contribute to the assessment of the justification of this investment. The possible payback of investment, time dedication that one would have to commit, as well as the presence of alternative forms of learning, should be taken into account.

Finally, the purpose of a gap analysis is to equip people with the skills to manage their career change with certainty. When career changers work within a systematic process of locating and fulfilling skill gaps, they may establish themselves as competitive in their new areas of work. This proactive strategy not only eases the transition process but also evokes a feeling of readiness and confidence when the individuals move to their new professional careers.

Chapter 5: Building Your Personal Brand

Crafting Your Career Change Narrative

The story that you create can become your most powerful weapon in the field of career change. It holds the authority to go beyond the normal scope of a resume or a cover letter, providing a glimpse of where not only you have been but also where you would like to be. It is the story that will connect all of your previous experiences, your present desires, and your future goals in a unified narrative that will appeal to prospective employers and industry gatekeepers.

The importance of the well-done narrative is based on the fact that it is able to answer and break the skepticism. You can turn possible skepticism into interest and involvement by creating a clear visual imagery of your experience and your inspirations. You should start the story by clearly stating your pivotal moment, the point that ushered you to the desire of change. This may be a self-revelation, a work situation, or a life experience that triggered a reconsideration of your professional course. When you place this moment as the launchpad to your new direction, you prepare the ground for an authentic and compelling narrative.

Organizing your career change narrative is a process whereby you map out a clear story arc. It can be done with the help of frameworks such as the "Problem-Pivot-Purpose" model, where you describe what in your previous job had you unhappy with (Problem), what had happened to you (Pivot) or a combination of things, which made you decide to change (Pivot), and what you are going to do (Purpose). This framework is not only clear but short and effective in telling your story.

It is important to find your why in the now moment. This deals with probing to the bottom to find the real reasons for your career shift. It can be motivated by a wish to do more rewarding work, the necessity to obtain a higher degree of freedom, or the desire to achieve a dream that has been long awaited, with this sense of urgency and purpose that you can make so persuasive by knowing and explaining why.

A different component is adapting your narrative to various audiences. You need to make your story audience and context-specific, whether you are networking, interviewing, or updating your LinkedIn profile. This could involve highlighting some things about your experience or varying the tone with the formality of the environment. As an example, a networking introduction could explore common interests or the problems faced in the industry. Still, a formal interview response could explore your strategic thinking and future objectives more.

After all, your career change story is not only about your description of the past; it is also about your future perspective. It is about putting yourself out there as an active, progressive person eager to make a contribution to your field of choice with new insights and a new vigor. A story that is both true and smart will help you lead to new possibilities and navigate the intricate path that a career change brings forth with surety.

Developing a Standout LinkedIn Profile

Developing a LinkedIn profile that helps define what your career change is all about is a strategic task that demands creativity and accuracy. Every part of your profile can be considered as a brick in the wall of building a story, which not only reflects on your previous accomplishments, but also indicates clearly what you are planning to do and what you will be able to do in the future.

Start with the headline - an area that is not valued much, yet it is important in creating the first impression. This must be a concise summary of what you are as a professional. Another way to think is to use a "bridge" headline to communicate what you are doing effectively and the course of your career change. An example is the name of the project, Project Manager / Operations Leader / Pivoting to Healthcare Tech: it lets any prospective professional know instantly about your experience and new direction.

The summary section is your time to tell a good story that responds to your career transformation. Begin with a first line that recognizes the change, calling on readers to know the motive and purpose of your expedition. This story must show how well your present and future goals can blend with all your prior experiences, and how your past experiences and jobs have made you fit to handle the new work. List here industry-specific keywords and skills, boosting your profile visibility in a search.

When explaining your experience, concentrate on the transferable skills and accomplishments that match your new career line. Note down bullet points to describe the measurable achievements. Make sure that the point is about skills that are applicable to your industry of interest. This is in addition to showing that you are valuable to the prospective employers; it gives them confidence that you will adapt and survive in your new environment.

The skills section is the critical element in maximizing the discoverability of your profile. Thorough research is necessary to determine what skills are most desired in your field of interest and reflect these in highlighting the top skills. Recommendations by colleagues can be valid; therefore, inquire with other former workmates or managers to confirm your listed skills.

Recommendations offer your strong social evidence and strengthen the story of your flexibility and capabilities. Solicit suggestions from those who are able to talk about your strengths and versatility, especially from those who have experienced your transition directly. The testaments must show traits that are immediately relevant to your new area of career interests.

Take advantage of the LinkedIn offers to improve the attractiveness of your profile. Turn on the Open to Work feature and indicate to recruiters that you are available and interested in new opportunities. Use the featured media section to highlight a portfolio work, presentations, or articles that demonstrate your professional identity in its developing manifestation. The creator mode option is also another way to increase your visibility, whereby you can post content and insights that will make you a thought leader in your new area.

Finally, the brilliant LinkedIn profile by a career switcher is the one that narrates a coherent story of development and opportunities. It must show a balance between the past and future goals, and it must be streamlined to the digital environment where first impressions matter. Considerably managing every aspect of your profile can enable you to convey your specific value proposition, with the help of which you will attract opportunities in accordance with your new direction in your professional activity.

Creating a Compelling Elevator Pitch

Development of a strong elevator pitch is important in the career change arena. This concise but impactful device acts as a connector between your past and your plans and goals, and briefly, with clarity, describes your professional identity and aspirations. An elevator pitch is not just a summary of your resume, but a story that displays passion and purpose, and it is formulated to attract attention and make an impression.

Suppose that you are on an elevator with a potential employer or networking contact, and all you have is the time it takes to get to the next level to make your introduction. This is your moment to shine, to define who you are, what you do, and where you are going in a succinct form. It must be audience-oriented and be specific to your audience group, be it peers in the industry, prospective employers, or networking specialists. Every variant of your pitch must be a bit different, which reflects the peculiarities of the case, as well as the interests of your listener.

Begin by finding out the important aspects that characterize your career. This encompasses your present or former job, the sectors that you have influenced, and the skills that you have acquired. Gradually move to your present career goals, showcasing the distinctiveness of value you can bring to the field of your choice. Not only should your pitch be about the successes that you experienced previously, but also your excitement about the new path that you are taking.

One of the most useful tricks to organize your pitch is a plain template: I am a former [job position] who assists [audience/industry] in accomplishing [result]. I am turning now to [new field] on the grounds of [reason]. Such a format will make sure that your pitch is straightforward, goal-oriented, and focused on your future. You must make your pitch flow easily and with confidence because only then can you deliver your speech with ease and authenticity.

Content is important as delivery. Your tone and body language ought to convey confidence, clarity, and enthusiasm. Connect with your listener by maintaining eye contact, making concentrating gestures, and using a calm and confident voice. Speak in front of the mirror, video record, and have your peers review your presentation.

Think of the situations where you may give your pitch. You can both network and make contacts at networking events, career fairs, and informal social gatherings. Alter your pitch to suit every situation so that it aligns with your audience and the location. As an example, a pitch at a career fair might be to highlight more of your qualifications and accomplishments, and a social introduction can be to highlight your passion and personal narrative.

The elevator pitch is not a tool fixed in stone, but it develops with you. The pitch must be updated as your career develops and experiences, skills, and aspirations evolve. It is crucial to rewrite and revise your pitch on a regular basis so that it can remain topical and convincing.

Finally, an elevator pitch that is well developed is an effective tool in the career transition arsenal. Not only does it convey your professional identity and objective, but it also creates confidence and new opportunities. When you learn to create an elevator pitch, you can better relate to people and improve your career in significant ways.

Building a Portfolio of Proof

Presenting the physical evidence of abilities is an important task in the sphere of career transition. A portfolio of evidence is an impressive witness to one's talents and accomplishments, which is much more impressive than a description of prior responsibilities. This is a collection of samples of work, case studies, and testimonials that form, after all, a powerful tool in proving one has the potential in a new field.

Such a portfolio can be built only by thoughtful choice and display of materials, which illuminate transferable achievements. Formats can be as diverse as PDFs and slide decks, or can be websites that belong to the owner, or projects that they can demonstrate. Every work in the portfolio is supposed to be a story of the path that one has taken, what was done, not only what was done, but what has been the difference, and what have been the outcomes.

An effective presentation deck can be used to give a summary of significant projects. In contrast, case studies may give a closer insight into a particular instance in which skills were utilized successfully. The performance metrics, the testimonials of any colleagues or clients, and the recommendations are all screenshots that add credibility layers to provide a full picture of the professional identity.

In addition to the conventional work experiences, the portfolio ought to utilize non-conventional sources as well. Relevant competencies can be illustrated through volunteer work or a passion project, where freelance work can be shown or demonstrations of ability in a variety of environments. An example of this is a non-profit fundraising event, which could be seen as an indication of marketing skills and a demonstration of the ability to motivate people and achieve outcomes.

The combination of these factors into job applications and interviews is itself a skill. Applicants are expected to talk about their portfolio effortlessly and use it to support their claims about their skills and their accomplishments. This can be facilitated through scripts and tips that would enable one to incorporate portfolio items in the discussion in a natural way. As an example, one could say, Let me demonstrate to you a project that I was leading a cross-functional team, thereby giving specific examples when talking about leadership skills.

Such a process of building a portfolio helps to seize new opportunities and deal with the digital footprint, which is of great importance. The rule of the day is to have a good online presence in the digital age. Some recruiters and hiring managers will tend to screen the candidates on the internet, where they expect uniformity and professionalism. This makes an online audit a required measure, so that the old or irrelevant data can be eliminated and the positive digital signals can be enhanced.

Bios-updating, membership in relevant online groups, and thought-leadership publication are all tactics to improve online presence. It is possible to write an article on LinkedIn about one's transition journey, such as emphasizing the intentional and conscious character of the career shift, and finding like-minded colleagues and possible opportunities to join industry-specific groups.

In essence, a portfolio of proof acts as a bridge between past experiences and future aspirations. It not only proves what one has managed to do but also preconditions what one is able to do in new positions. Through careful gathering and demonstration of evidence of abilities and achievements, career changers can also convince potential employers about their willingness and potential to succeed in the new discipline.

Chapter 6: Mastering the Modern Job Search

Reverse-Engineering Job Descriptions

When changing careers, learning how to best match skills and experiences with the requirements of the prospective employers is one of the most important steps to take. This starts with learning the art of reverse-engineering job descriptions, a strategic move that empowers career changers to customize their applications to fit certain market requirements.

Job postings must be carefully analyzed, and this is the first step of this process. Every job description is a goldmine of information and defines the desired skills and duties, as well as, in many cases, what is expected of the position, even though it is not written down. In breaking down these components, career changers are able to build a target profile that is quantifiable to the role they hope to win. This includes color-coding qualifications in the posting of samples to avoid confusion between qualifications that they must have and those that are not absolutely required. This type of visual disaggregation assists in ranking the skills and experience to emphasize in applications.

Having identified the main necessities of a job, the next thing to do is to match personal experience to those requirements. This is the process of creating literal links between transferable skills and job requirements. A useful aid in the process can be the development of a matrix of personal experiences versus job description bullet points so that every application can be customized to accentuate the best bits of the candidate's background.

Much of this analysis is associated with making sense of the most important "code words" and industry lingo that is interwoven in job descriptions. Such terms are commonly a pointer to the soft skills and cultural fit that an employer is pursuing, but not necessarily defining. Knowledge of popular keywords in certain industries, including technology, healthcare, and nonprofit organisations, can be an advantage in creating applications that appeal to hiring managers.

Moreover, such reverse-engineering methodology is not only useful in applications but also in interviews. Candidates quickly learn how to be more prepared to talk about their experiences in a manner that fits the requirements of the employer by learning the language and expectations of a job description. In order to make the process of a candidate attractive in a project management position, when we consider an example like transforming a role in which one is being called as a managed classroom, leading cross-functional teams, may be enough.

The final aim of reverse-engineering job descriptions is to make sure that career changers are able to tell their stories in a manner that will be appealing to employees and show them that their unusual background can be used to fulfill the needs of a new industry. Not only does such a tactical convergence increase the chance of securing interviews, but it also creates a feeling of certainty that the job seeker will successfully transfer to a new area.

Lastly, reverse-engineering job descriptions is also a viable process that job applicants can employ to fit their accounts into the new job. Career changers can easily make themselves the best fit in the job they want by properly analyzing job ads, mapping their experiences against the job specifications, and mastering industry language. This kind of orderly method for job applications makes a job-seeker more appealing and provides an excellent introduction to the confusing realm of career transitions.

Writing a Career Changer's Resume

A career changer needs to revise their resume, meaning to write the resume strategically to reveal the transferable skills and relevant experiences. In particular, the common chronological resume format might not serve a useful purpose in demonstrating the variety of what you can do when your work starts to focus on a different direction. Hybrid or functional forms are suggested instead because they focus more on skills and achievements rather than on a chronological job record. This will enable you to tell a coherent story that supports your new career objective.

It is very important to have a good professional summary on the first page of the resume. In this section, you should briefly explain what your career pivot is and what you are looking to do. It acts as a preview to potential employers, and shows what you are motivated by and what you are contributing to the table. Be able to use language that will tie your previous life to your future goals and clearly explain how your history will be useful in your new career.

Individual keywords are crucial to having your resume noticed, particularly with Applicant Tracking Systems (ATS). Take a critical look at job postings in your field of interest to determine and use industry-specific words and language. This is typically done not only to pass through the ATS filters but also to demonstrate that you are familiar with the jargon and expectations of the industry.

Describe the work experience, paying much attention to achievements, not to responsibilities. The key to organizing your bullet points in a STAR (Situation-Task-Action-Result) system is to make sure that each bullet point includes an example of a required skill or achievement. Measureable accomplishments are especially effective because they give tangible proof of what you can do and what changes you create.

There is also some creativity needed in paraphrasing past positions into new industry language when building a resume as a career changer. This could include rewording previous job titles or duties to be more in line with what is expected of your desired job. To use a classroom example, you might call this led cross-functional teams to appeal to project management functions.

You should also make your resume specific to your application. This may sound time-consuming, but tailoring your resume to match the needs and culture of a specific employer can greatly advance your chances of securing an interview. Focus on the qualifications and experience that are the most relevant to the job, and modify the tone and priorities of the organization to suit your language.

Along with the resume, you can also consider creating a portfolio of your work and achievements. This may be especially useful in transitioning into creative or technical careers, where examples of your work can speak volumes about your abilities and capabilities.

Finally, a career changer resume needs to be a good story of development and promise. It makes the case for how your previous experiences, competencies, and accomplishments make you particularly well-positioned to address the emerging issues you want to work on. Contrasting what you offer to the new field and being able to explain it easily and convincingly can help you make a compelling case to support your candidacy and unlock new and exciting career prospects.

Beating the ATS

Searching and navigating the digital side of job applications can be an overwhelming process, especially using Applicant Tracking Systems (ATS). These systems, which are meant to make the recruitment process easier, tend to become iron gates separating the candidates from the job they want. Learning their mechanics is one of the key elements that any career changer should be aware of to make a successful transition.

Applicant Tracking Systems are basically computer applications that can help automate the recruitment procedure by screening out resumes even before they reach human hands. They sort resumes based on keywords, formats, and structures that are relevant to the job description. The main role of such systems is to make the work of the recruiter easier by reducing the number of job applicants to those whose resumes closely match the job requirements. But that, in turn, implies that even highly qualified candidates might still be passed over, unless their resumes are optimized against such systems.

The initial stage in defeating the ATS is learning how to make your resume look the part. Do not use graphics, tables, or unusual fonts, because the parsing software may misinterpret these. Instead, stick to a clean, simple layout with clear headings such as "Experience" and "Education." Make sure that all sections are easily recognisable and that they make sense. Such simplicity makes the ATS read and decipher your resume content correctly.

Another important strategy is the inclusion of the correct keywords. Such keywords need to reflect the language used in the job description. To explain, where project management is mentioned as a qualification in the job advert, ensure you include this particular wording in your resume. This will not only help to get your resume past the ATS filters but will also demonstrate to your prospective employers that you are well-informed and fit the job requirements.

In addition, look at the strategic location of your main competencies. Having them at the top of your resume will instantly send out signals to the ATS and the hiring managers. This method has the additional advantage of not only emphasizing your best skills but also maximizing the likelihood of such skills being harvested in the first scan.

It can be a priceless exercise to check if your resume fits with ATS. Jobscan or ResumeWorded is not the only available tool; many are free or paid, which will allow you to estimate how much your resume matches ATS requirements. These are sites that allow you to get some information about where you need to improve, so that you can perfect your document.

Along with the resume, a specially designed cover letter can be very important as well. In the case of career changers, the cover letter can be used to explain your pivot to the prospective employer and make a strong case as to why your prior experience would apply in the new job. Breaking down the link between the present and the past will help you alleviate some fears that might arise due to your unconventional background.

Finally, the key to success in using the ATS is a strategic format, key keyword optimization, and practice. By doing so, career changers are likely to increase their likelihood of not only overcoming these digital gatekeepers but also impressing their potential employers. Such planning and forethought can be the difference between the successful and the unsuccessful transition into a new career domain.

Crafting Tailored Cover Letters

A cover letter is an important job change tool in this market, providing a special arena in which one area challenges the complexities of another. Not only is it lip service, but it is also a strategic document that allows those in need of jobs to bridge the gap between the past and the future. The cover letter is a story that bridges the gap between past and future in the life of a candidate and is a personal touch that a resume lacks.

When it comes to writing a personalized cover letter, the first step is to know why a cover letter is required. In contrast to a generic application, a cover letter to career changers should clearly answer the question of why the change is being pursued and how the experience obtained in the past fits the new position. This is not the question of simply listing the competencies; this is a question of developing a story that embodies survival and imagination. The introduction paragraph ought to be a hook, a reason that the reader wants to hear why the career shift happened. To make the example work, a former teacher can say that they are shifting their orientation towards project management, they are also accustomed to working in cross-functional teams, and this immediately translates into what type of skills they will require in the new work environment.

Within the body of the letter, the applicant needs to work on connecting his/her transferable skills to the employer. This is not only recognizing the applicable skills but also giving examples. Suppose that a person has left a job in the field of healthcare and has gone to work in the data analysis field; he or she may inform you how he or she was able to develop his or her analytical skills working on healthcare data and improving patient outcomes. Through these parallels, the cover letter emerges as a compelling story that gives potential employers confidence that the candidate is able to adjust and thrive in a new setting.

Another important element is to respond to possible counterarguments. Candidates must take the initiative to identify any gaps or perceived drawbacks in their background. In this way, they can put any form of doubt that may be in the mind of the reader to rest. One would be when one abandons an area of creativity for a technical one and notices a learning curve, but he/she balances it out by writing about his/her self-studies or the courses he/she took to fill in the gap.

The cover letter must end with a call to action to get the employer to get in touch. This could involve a request to interview or a proposal to explain how the individual background of the candidate can be used to the advantage of the company. Finishing with a statement of confidence and excitement supports the candidate in her dedication to the transition and the desire to apply her various skills to the new position.

Finally, the best cover letter to use as a career changer is not simply one that restates a resume. It is narrative--the art of creating a coherent story that makes sense of the past and future, meets the requirements and opportunities of a career transition. With careful self-positioning, applicants are able to turn their cover letter into a strong case to explain why they are the right employee in a new industry, increasing their likelihood of a successful transition.

Chapter 7: Interviewing as a Career Switcher

Anticipating and Answering Tough Questions

The process of career change requires both bravery and careful planning in order to navigate the stormy sea of change. The expectation of rigorous questions during the interview is one of the most frightening issues career switchers face. These questions typically cover the causes of the change occurrence, the relevance of the former experience and knowledge, or experience gaps. All these questions are questions of comprehension, and getting ready to respond will become an opportunity to demonstrate the ability to be confident and flexible.

The key to sailing through these interviews is the preparation of the questions exploring the why of the career shift. The interviewers will have a natural curiosity as to why there is a major shift in career direction. Why are you making this change? These are some of the questions. These are formalities, but crucial tests of sanity and faith in the transition. Are common. A systematic approach allows a rational explanation of the connections between present achievements and the opportunities in the future in order to demonstrate that changing careers is no capricious choice.

Making a response that is both genuine and strategic can be very important.

These questions are best addressed using the frameworks of responses. One of the effective tools in this respect is the SAR (Situation-Action-Result) tool. Through this framework, candidates are able to present their previous experiences in a manner that demonstrates the applicability and transferability of their skills to the new job. In addition to that, this skepticism, based on the perceived overqualification or a lack of experience, must be overcome.

The reactions might include highlighting the idea that the relationships with and among customers that had to be managed in a previous job could be directly transferred into new work, which helps to justify the relevance of various experiences. The interviewers may raise the issue of overqualification or how fast a person can change to a new industry. This is where reframing is involved. Rather than seeing a deficiency in direct experience as a weakness, it can be offered as a new point of view with new ideas and methods on the table. At this stage of preparation, peer feedback and mock interviews are useful.

Acting out the methods included in the interview, such as a peer interview swap, will help the applicant sharpen his responses and gain confidence. It will help the applicant to perfect his responses and gain confidence by practicing the techniques involved in the interview, such as a peer interview swap. Simulated interviews are a safe environment to practice various stories and get constructive feedback, which is highly important in developing the skill of responding to unexpected questions gracefully.

Basically, the key to predicting and responding to challenging questions during career change interviews is to tell a story that is interesting and believable. It entails transforming what may be seen as areas of weakness into strengths and showing a sense of direction for what lies ahead. With a well-planned process, structured frameworks, and intensive practice, career changers will be more likely to approach the interview with confidence and poise and use possible obstacles as an opportunity to demonstrate individual value to the employer.

Handling Skepticism and Curveballs

Life is full of doubts in search of a career change. It frequently comes both outside and inside, and questions one's decision and sense of direction. Skepticism may be both peripheral, as in the way others might view the wisdom of quitting a secure job to pursue an uncertain business, or central, in which self-doubt and fear of the unknown cast a pall over the path. These suspicions need to be tactfully handled with a combination of preparation, endurance, and tactics.

The trick in an interview or networking with someone who questions you is to make your story sound like the truth and understand it. Put into words your reasons why you want to change, pointing out the consistency of what has happened to you in the past with what is happening to you today. Apply systematic models, like the STAR approach (Situation, Task, Action, Result), to explain how your previous job experiences have prepared you with universal skills that have been applied to your new profession. This will not only help to convince potential employers of your ability, but it will also help to remind you of your potential to excel in the new environment.

On the inside, the management of skepticism is the identification and restructuring of constraining beliefs. These assumptions usually take the form of arguments such as I am too old to switch careers or I lack the experience. To refute them, compile a list of your achievements and the competencies you have mastered that can be used in any industry. It will help to reorient your thinking away from doubt and towards possibility and potential by regularly thinking about these accomplishments.

Another aspect of career change that has to be dealt with is curveballs. They can be surprise questions during interviews, surprise barriers to new work, or surprise personal situations that work to your advantage in your transition. Curveball control level depends upon training and flexibility. The Interview Preparation involves predicting challenging questions and coming up with answers that make perceived weaknesses look like strengths. An example of this is transforming a shortage of first-hand experience into a new way of seeing or a chance to introduce something new to the table.

Flexibility is essential regarding the use of curve balls in new activities. Accept change as something that will always be there and see every obstacle as a learning and growth experience. This attitude not only eases the present-day situation but also develops the strength to overcome the problems that lie ahead. Moreover, building a network of mentors, peers, and industry contacts can be helpful in offering guidance and encouragement in times of unforeseen setbacks.

And finally, it comes down to dealing with skepticism and curveballs, which is to have a clear picture of what you want to achieve, and to be ready to explain it and justify it. It is about creating a story that links your past to your future, and illustrating what you can add to new opportunities. It is also about inculcating a sense of being receptive to learning, adjusting to failures, and perceiving them as stumbling blocks rather than obstacles.

These are the very strategies that can turn skepticism to support and curveballs into growth triggers, such that your career change process becomes efficient, motivating, and empowering concurrently.

Mock Interview Exercises

Think about entering a room where the air smells of some anticipation and nerves, a space that many people who are about to make a career change would feel at home. This is where the focus is on you, when you are ready to demonstrate your capabilities and potential during a simulation interview. Not only drilling, but a strategy towards a new career path is sure and precise.

The mock interviews are a great method to mimic the situation of the interview, practice answering questions in real life, and train your skills to tell a story. When working in this controlled setting, you are advised to express your experiences, prowess, and ambitions and create stories that potential employers can relate to. It does not simply matter to practice the answers, work out the art of communication, and the ways of becoming part of a great story, but also what you have accomplished earlier to be able to use it in your future job.

In such exercises, you are challenged to investigate different types of questions. These are behavioral questions that examine the past via inquiries like the STAR (Situation-Task-Action-Result) model and situational questions, which identify the ability and versatility of issue-solving. The answers to these questions will enable you to know what you are good at and what you can work on; hence, when responding, you will produce genuine responses that are also strategic to the job you are seeking.

In addition, mock interviews provide an opportunity to obtain useful feedback during peer or mentor reviews. This is very valuable feedback, in that you can see how your responses are viewed and how you can change them to be clearer and effective. With this feedback in place, you not only become better at refining your responses but also at becoming more confident by learning to be poised in a highly stressful situation.

These exercises may be expanded beyond the individual to include peer-to-peer swaps of interviews. This dynamic gives the opportunity to have a dual viewpoint: being on both sides of the table during the interview process. By playing the role of the interviewer, you know what the employers want, and being the interviewee helps to sharpen your skills in responding. This two-way learning experience not only gives you an in-depth insight into the dynamics of the interview, but it also builds your empathy, which is essential in any work environment.

One more way of countering anxiety related to real interviews is by including mock interviews in your training plan. Getting used to the format and being exposed to the kind of questions you will encounter will help you feel less uncertain about the process and, therefore, more confident about the real interviews. The practice keeps you exercised and turns the nerves into performance energy.

Finally, mock interview practice is about getting you the skills and confidence to be successful in the interview realm. What you ought to remember during these simulations is that each session will be an investment in your career. A strategy to make a good candidate out of you can help you make a good premise for a change of career by taking the feedback on board and optimizing your strategy to become a strong candidate to reach the next stage in your career progress.

Salary Negotiation Conversations

The art of navigating the complex dance of salary negotiation is an important skill in the repertoire of any career changer. Compensation debate is not about getting a financial package, but about values alignment, value recognition, and creating a platform on which to build a new career path. This starts by ensuring he conducts in-depth research not just about the standard salary scales in the new industry, but also about the individual factors that could affect the compensation package, including location, size of the company, and growth trends in the industry.

Salary negotiation is a matter that needs to be approached strategically. Demystifying the procedure of salary research has to be performed first using various sources. Glassdoor, Payscale, LinkedIn, and other websites provide good information on industry standards. These sites offer points of reference that can assist a career changer in seeing where they are located in the pay scale and shifting their expectations accordingly. It is good to note that a move to a new area may involve a short-term reduction in salary, which must be considered against the prospective promotions and non-financial rewards that could make the whole experience more rewarding.

Armed with information, the second step is to get ready to actually talk. This includes development of answers to frequently asked questions like What did you make before? and "What are you seeking now?" When changing professions, it is important to put these responses in a context that could show the importance of new skills and experiences. An example would be, I would say, based on my recent career change and the research I have done, a fair salary range would be... Not only does this demonstrate preparedness, it also demonstrates confidence in the value one will add to the new position.

A negotiation is more about what is said than what is not said. This is especially useful with the so-called pause and counter technique, where one listens critically, waits a moment to think, and then replies thoughtfully. This is good to keep leverage and show a cool, composed attitude. Another important thing is to know when to run when the offer falls short of the minimum specifications or when the negotiation process is at a dead end.

Other than money, non-monetary benefits must be discussed in the negotiation. Available work flexibility, professional development, and health benefits are all relevant elements of a compensation package. During these discussions, a list of desired benefits can come in handy, where all the elements of the offer are taken into account.

It can be a useful practice to negotiate a role-playing situation with a peer or mentor. This type of role-playing discussion can be used in real life to focus on plans and develop confidence. Also, knowing some pitfalls and avoiding them might make a real difference. Negotiation can be more likely to work when it is approached as a strategy with established goals, a sense of your own worth, and a desire to come to a win-win solution.

Salary negotiation is, however, not just a financial transaction but a conversation that determines whether one enters a new industry. It is concerned with self-advocacy and recognizing the context of the career change. Career changers can achieve success not only in getting paid but also in getting a job that matches their career goals and personal ethics through preparing, being confident, and being strategic.

Chapter 8: Life Integration: Family, Finances, and Well-Being

The Family Conversation

There is a sense of anticipation, an unofficial tension that tends to surround major transformations in life as people sit at the dinner table. The only audible sound is the clanging of knives and forks, as the individual family members ponder the conversation to come. The choice of career change is not a one-person process, but it permeates the family, changes the relationships, disrupts habits, and evokes emotions.

Such a conversation must commence very delicately and yet decisively to provide a platform where candor and compassion can thrive. The person considering the pivot needs to be ready to explain his or her vision not only in the framework of his or her own dreams but also within the scope of the family as a whole. It is about creating a story that includes not just the possible dangers involved but also the common aspirations that are yet to be achieved.

The challenge is to understand that there are fears to be considered as the words start to move. Financial security is usually first on the agenda, the bogeyman that towers large over career change. The problem with this anxiety is not simply in numbers and finances but in providing the loved ones with the confidence that the leap into the unknown is a well-considered one, that the safety nets are in place, and that the path is hard to predict, but not suicidal.

Children with all their innocent curiosity may not understand the idea of changing careers, particularly when it is associated with meeting a parent more or less often at home. Here, the discussion turns into a teaching moment, describing what work is like in terms they can relate to, and maybe even including them in insignificant but encouraging ways.

The practicality of such a change or its timing may be challenged by the extended family with their own expectations and experience. It is here that the skill to listen is of the highest order, to receive their views, and to respond subtly to the logic of the decision. It is a word and emotion game, and it attempts to transform the uncertainties into motivation.

It is not a strategy to include family values and goals in this discussion, but it is a necessity. It demands an inquiry into what each of the family members truly values, and the change in career is adjusted according to those values. The tools would facilitate the interaction of the values, and a family values worksheet would help to cement the concepts and to ensure that the pivot was not only facilitating individual growth, but a healthy family as well.

Movement and purchase require continuous talking. Holding frequent check-ins where every member has the opportunity to express themselves and their concerns will serve to keep the communication channels open. These meetings act as a sounding board and a milestone celebration, which helps to enforce the notion that this change is a family project.

This discussion is ultimately more than a career shift; it is also like stitching a new chapter in the family story. It concerns the realization that, however the role of an individual may fluctuate, the family always stays the same; it evolves and develops along with it. Using empathy, you can envision the family not only as supportive but also as re-energized by the opportunities the future holds.

Financial Planning for Career Change

Switching careers is an exciting, yet fearful undertaking, and one of the first things that many worry about is financial security. To make this transition, it would be important to create a sound financial plan. Career change financial planning is anchored on a thorough knowledge of your financial situation today and careful planning of the financial issues awaiting you in the future.

It is advisable to start with an evaluation of your financial runway. This includes calculating how much money you will spend to live, and how many years you can live without a regular income, depending on your savings. A comprehensive spreadsheet of your budget can aid you in planning your necessary expenditures versus unnecessary expenses so that you can find where you can save. To prevent any ugly surprises, it is always important to have a clear picture of what you are spending each month and how much you have saved to spend.

Another key step is to build a transition fund. This fund serves as a financial cushion to give you comfort as you negotiate the ambiguities of a career transition. Begin by looking at what you are already saving and think about how to increase it. This may include cutting back on your costs of living, deferring unnecessary non-essential expenditure, or seeking temporary employment to supplement your earnings. The aim of this is to establish a safety net so that you move on with your career change without worrying every time that you are going to run out of money.

Your financial strategy will consist of risk management and contingency planning. You should have a backup plan in case the worst happens. This may involve finding possible side hustles or part-time employment that matches your skills and interests, providing you with financial stability and an opportunity to learn something new. Also, an emergency fund checklist can help you put aside money that can be used exclusively when there is an unexpected expense that you may have to meet during your transition.

Insurance and benefits are things that are easily ignored, yet are crucial when changing careers. The lack of employer-provided benefits means that you have to find alternatives to health insurance, like COBRA or ACA. Likewise, think about how to maintain contributions to retirement and other benefits during any periods of unemployment. Making changes to your beneficiary details and learning what your insurance means are two steps that should not be overlooked.

Bridge gigs and side hustles may also ease your financial load and offer emotional relief in this time frame. Such short-term sources of income may be used to alleviate the stress of a career change, providing flexibility and an opportunity to explore new areas. Whenever selecting side hustles, ensure that they align with your career future goals to gain the relevant experience and skills.

Finally, stress and burnout management will help you stay healthy in general. Financial insecurity can result in a high level of stress, and it can be helpful to include mindfulness exercises and stress management methods in your routine. This helps to control your emotions but also improves your ability to concentrate and make decisions throughout your career changeover.

Finally, a career change can be achieved successfully with a carefully designed financial plan that allows you to move forward and explore new opportunities confidently and clearly.

Exploring Side Hustles and Bridge Gigs

With the changing nature of the employment landscape, the idea of side hustles and bridge gigs is becoming even more topical. These other types of work provide a reasonable alternative way to earn an income and acquire valuable experience in transitioning to a new career. They provide some cushioning against the financial risk that a full career change can sometimes entail, and they can enable individuals to explore new industries and jobs without fear of immediate success.

Freelance work, consulting work, or gig economy jobs are not only about earning extra income, but they are also a strategic move to improve skills and build professional networks. To use this as an illustration, a marketing professional struggling to break into tech may consider freelance writing on behalf of tech companies. This not only keeps the money coming but also gains some experience and contacts within the industry of choice.

Bridge gigs, however, are temporary jobs that are used as stepping stones to a new career. The positions provide an opportunity to explore new industries or job roles without any long-term commitment. They enable people to explore other areas, evaluate their suitability, and make sound judgments on their future course of action. An example is when a person who wants to be involved in education technology takes an online tutoring job to see what the industry dynamics are like before getting into it.

Determining the right side hustles or bridge gigs is something that needs to be approached intelligently. It is a process in which one balances these roles with their overall career objectives, present competencies, and desired competencies. This process may be facilitated by a decision matrix that can help to measure opportunities by their time commitment and income potential and align them with future goals.

It also requires being a planner and a manager to start a side hustle or a bridge job. These roles need to be maintained with other roles so that one avoids burnout. Some of the tips that can be applied practically, depending on the given job, are setting a clear boundary, negotiating a reasonable salary, and using tools to monitor time and money. Platforms such as Upwork or Fiverr may be an ideal place to start when seeking freelance opportunities. In contrast, job boards or networking based on specific industries may result in more profitable bridge jobs.

In addition, it is necessary to cope with the stress and uncertainty associated with having many roles. It can support mental health by adding mindfulness activities that may include meditation or journaling. This can be monitored by regular check-ins with individual goals and progress to ensure such roles are continuing to be productive and in line with overall career goals.

In general, side hustles and bridge jobs are no longer a one-time deal; they are included in an overall career transition strategy. They give people a chance to be in charge of their career, providing them with financial security and the opportunity to discover and experiment with new, exciting directions.

Managing Stress and Uncertainty

Stress and uncertainty become the dark clouds obscuring the path in the career change labyrinth. These factors, although overwhelming, are part of the transformation process as they are the challenge as well as the stimuli. Knowing how to sail through these rough seas is essential to anybody who decides to change careers.

Career change is an emotive phase that is characterized by both excitement and nervousness. There is nothing unusual in being overwhelmed by the thought of making the first step into the unknown, where what one is used to doing is giving way to the unknown and unexplored. Such doubt can be a breeding ground of anxiety that is reflected in immediate sleepless nights and anxious days full of doubt. The first step of managing these feelings is to recognize them as a normal aspect of the transition.

Mindfulness is one of the strategies that can be used to reduce stress. This includes entering the moment one is living in, not judging thoughts and emotions, and letting go of the stress that uncertainty can cause. Deep breathing exercises, meditation, and mindful walking are just a few techniques that can be applied as anchors, giving clarity and peace during a chaotic time. Not only do the practices alleviate stress, but they also enhance concentration and emotional endurance to overcome challenges with a healthy mind.

A routine can also be stabilizing. A sense of order can be introduced into the uncertainty of career change by developing a systematic plan that incorporates time to reflect, learn, and rest. It is the routine that serves as a guide to work with, and the sense of being lost is then diminished, and the person feels more in control of the surrounding world.

In addition, a support network should be developed. Mentoring, peer support groups, or online forums can provide a needed boost and perspective. These links not only provide useful pieces of advice but also bring to the minds of those who are struggling that they are not the only ones. Being able to share experiences and learn about other people who have been through some of the same transitions can give confidence and encouragement to persevere.

In addition to the emotional support, practical coping skills in dealing with uncertainty include realistic goal setting and flexibility. By taking a big target and making it smaller, achievable steps help the individual develop a sequence of wins, which creates momentum and makes the task not as daunting as it might seem. The flexibility, in turn, enables adapting to unexpected situations and transforming all possible failures into sources of development and education.

By taking uncertainty as a friend instead of an enemy, the journey of career change can become a new one. Every moment of uncertainty is a chance to understand oneself better, to become more resilient, and to become better at solving problems. When seeing uncertainty in this way, people will move beyond the fear mindset and into one of curiosity and exploration.

Lastly, all of the career change stress/management is about finding a balance. It concerns both accepting the difficulties and also accepting the opportunities for personal and professional development that are present in them. The road to a new career can be a discovery and an empowerment process that can create not only a different but also a very fulfilling future with the right strategies and mindset.

Chapter 9: Time Management for Busy Professionals

Micro-Stepping to Progress

The concept of progress may easily become overwhelming in the quest to change careers, especially with the pressure of living a busy life. The micro-stepping principle does, however, offer a radical approach, as it merely breaks down big jobs into small, manageable steps. This approach destroys the myth according to which progress must be made with great gestures or with great investments of time. Rather, it embraces the virtues of micro-actions that can bring about significant change.

To those who are overwhelmed by the thought of redefining their careers, micro-stepping is a plan that fits even the most strict of schedules. It promotes the use of short-run, focused interventions as part of everyday life. One such power session is 15 minutes of job seeking or skill building that can accumulate to huge gains over time. Not only does this style fit well into a busy schedule, but it also helps to sustain the pace and drive.

Time-blocking and batching are two of the most important strategies in micro-stepping. People can improve their efficiency and concentration by dedicating a certain amount of time to work and by grouping tasks that are similar to each other. This may include reserving an afternoon to conduct information interviews or investing a weekend to upskill by taking courses online. A minute can be a treasure, even with such a structured plan, and burnout will be less common as people will feel a sense of accomplishment.

Micro-stepping also includes reflection and adaptation. This can be done by periodically evaluating what strategies have worked and what needs to be fixed to improve a strategy continuously. Weekly reflection prompts or worksheets that show what worked/what didn't can support it, since they may aid in establishing a proactive approach to self-development and time management. Action, reflection, and adjustment are important cyclical processes that help keep the trajectory moving forward.

However, development is not only about personal achievement. Establishing accountability mechanisms can also play a big role in increasing one's dedication to micro-stepping. It requires the push or pull [peer support, mentorship, or self-tracking tools] to keep the momentum going. Progress tracking templates or establishing regular check-ins with an accountability partner may present the support structure required to be on track.

Another principle of the micro-stepping strategy is celebrating small wins. A positive feedback loop is generated when one motivates oneself to value the purchase of milestones, no matter how minor. It adds importance to persistence and perseverance, and helps not to give up and be enthusiastic. These festivities may be minor, like snacking on a favorite food or sharing stories of success with an encouraging crowd.

Finally, the fact that a career change is not a marathon but a sprint is hinted at in the idea of micro-stepping forward. It states that the major change can be realized through small, gradual steps that are possible to implement in the context of everyday life. Through this approach, people can manage the challenges encountered during a career shift with ease and accuracy as they understand that every little step will bring them nearer to their end objectives.

Building Accountability Systems

When it comes to career change, having a strong accountability system is the key to keeping the ball rolling and achieving long-term growth. Accountability captures this quality because it focuses on putting intentions into action, which gives us a framework that helps us through the complexities of moving careers.

Self-awareness and realization of the need to set realistic and attainable goals are the starting point of accountability. It is a process that requires the development of a stepwise plan that includes a set of milestones and deadlines that act as physical indicators of advances. This kind of plan helps not only to guide but also to motivate people to stick with the change they want to make.

In order to successfully develop accountability, it is necessary to include both internal and external motivators. Internal motivators tend to be pushed by personal goals and the innate need to get better. Nevertheless, these internal motivators can be supported by external motivators. Here, the force of community and peer support may be seen. It can be extremely encouraging and constructive to talk to a group of people who are experiencing career transitions and have shared thoughts on the subject. Making routine contact with accountability partners or groups fosters a sense of camaraderie and purpose that may be incredibly motivating.

Digital tools and resources further enhance accountability systems. Apps and platforms that are built to track goals and monitor progress can assist people in becoming better organized and focused. The Course, progress tracker, and milestones features can help keep you on track. These devices provide live information regarding a person's progress and give the opportunity to make certain changes and improvements in strategies in a timely manner.

In addition, it is crucial to implement reflection and self-assessment into the accountability system. Regular self-assessment enables a person to assess his or her performance, identify positive outcomes, and determine where to go. The habit creates a growth mentality, which promotes never-ending learning and change. It is also important to celebrate small wins as it promotes confidence and the idea that progress is being made, albeit in small steps.

Other elements that can greatly enhance an accountability system are mentorship and peer accountability. Developing networks with mentors who have successfully made the same transition can offer a sense of direction, perspective, and support. Mentors may provide a new way of looking and may assist in recognizing areas of blindness, so that the person is not derailed by his/her objectives.

Motivation and commitment can also be improved by adding rewards for meeting milestones. The rewards do not necessarily have to be lavish; they can be modest rewards of advancement, like a day off or doing something a person loves. The important thing is to make sure that the rewards have meaning and are in line with personal values.

The rewards are high, and the level of commitment needed to build an accountability system is high. By establishing a system of tracking progress, communication with supportive communities, and using digital solutions, individuals can create a robust framework that can not only assist them in the process of transitioning to a new profession but also promote personal and professional growth. Finally, accountability systems enable individuals to own their process and turn dreams into real accomplishments.

Setting Milestones and Celebrating Micro-Wins

Taking a career change as a rather complicated task, the creation of some milestones is one of the most basic building blocks of keeping the course and ensuring motivation. When they divide the big career objectives into smaller and manageable ones, people can easily navigate the overwhelming transition process with more clarity and confidence. These milestones are not the only path map, but they also act as a way to decide how far the transformation is going, and amend the strategies where the need arises.

Milestone setting starts with a careful definition of both short-term, mid-term, and long-term objectives. The short-term goals may be to finish certain training packages or to expand personal network, and the mid-term goals may be to get a job in the preferred field. Long-term goals, like getting to the top of the ladder and becoming a leader or starting their own business, are a far-off but promising vision that feeds perseverance.

Milestones are so powerful because they help to make a daunting career change seem like a sequence of manageable steps to follow. This division has the added benefit of making the transition less overwhelming but more focused and determined. Every milestone that one attains is a brick that helps to build the foundation on which other milestones are built. The smaller achievements that people cross off on their lists enable them to develop a sense of real-life achievement that enhances self-efficacy and motivation.

Along with the establishment of milestones, it is important to celebrate the micro-wins. These minor wins, which are sometimes not significant when viewed through the large lens of the game, can be very useful in keeping morale and momentum going. Micro-wins may be as small as finishing a successful informational interview or getting positive feedback on a new skill mastered. Having known these achievements, however slight they might be, leads to a positive psychological state and further effort.

Micro-wins can be celebrated in a wide variety of ways, including as a personal reward (e.g., treating oneself to a favorite snack after a successful day) or sharing successes with a supportive community. These rewards of recognition act as inspirational supports and remind people of their achievement and their potential. In addition, they give them a chance to reflect, enabling career changers to examine what is working and where corrections may be necessary.

A culture of positivity and resilience is also developed through the practice of micro-wins. Greater attention to what has already been accomplished as opposed to what still needs accomplishment can help individuals stay in a forward-looking perspective that is crucial in the process of overcoming the many obstacles that come with a career change. This move towards the positive (strengths) rather than the negative (deficits) fosters an adaptive mind that is vital to long-term success.

In brief, the two-fold approach to career change learning, i.e., setting milestones and celebrating micro-wins, is a useful means of learning to change careers. The combination of the two offers the framework and the motivation needed to ensure a successful transition through the various challenges it presents. In this way, the career changers will have the opportunity to make the insurmountable mission look like a series of steps that are to be accomplished, and the accomplishment of which is marked by a reward and a lesson in itself. They will eventually lead to a rewarding new stage of their professional life.

Navigating the First 90 Days in a New Role

A new role has a critical period that marks the beginning of success. It is these 90 days that will be crucial in developing a good ground, which will result in the development and assimilation of the new environment. It is an exciting and difficult time as one learns the subtleties of a new work culture, develops a relationship, and realizes what is expected of them in a particular position.

This transition would be greatly assisted by a systematic method. It can be useful to create a 30-60-90 day plan. The plan should indicate the goals of each phase, which will be useful not only in concentrating the efforts but also in assessing the development. The initial 30 days need to focus on learning and observation. It is a period to take in as much information as possible about the company operations, culture, and people. Recording notes at meetings, posing questions, and requesting peer feedback may be a great source of information.

Another success factor in a new position is relationship building. Focus on building relationships with the key stakeholders and team members. Begin individual meetings (telephone, coffee, lunch, etc.) to get to know their roles and expectations. Not only do these interactions concern the acquisition of information, but they also concern the development of rapport and the show of interest.

Relationship-building should be proactive to facilitate the process of becoming a part of the team and create avenues to cooperate with the team.

It is also important to learn the unwritten workplace rules. Practically, any organization has its own culture and norms that are never clearly described but are vital in order to fit in. It may help to monitor how other people in the organization interact, dress, and resolve conflicts. Such nuances can be detected, and this may prevent misunderstanding and help to make the behavior part of the company culture.

Errors during the initial stages are normal and must be regarded as a way to learn. A steep learning curve is normal, and the valence of resiliency matters. Look at feedback as an opportunity to improve the skills and methods. A desire to obtain feedback on supervisors and colleagues can also indicate an interest in change and flexibility.

Life-long learning and continuous improvement are essential to success. Early detection of gaps in skills and filling them with courses or mentorship could help to improve performance and job satisfaction. Monitoring of progress and setting of learning goals is one method of sustaining the course of personal development as dictated by the professional world.

The first 90 days of a new position revolve around the art of learning and giving. It includes knowing the terrain, establishing relationships, and laying the groundwork for future success. With curiosity, openness, and planning, it is possible to establish a good foundation towards a successful and satisfying time at his new office.

Chapter 10: Continuous Learning and Upskilling

Identifying Skill Gaps and Growth Areas

When it comes to career changes, clearly knowing the skill gaps and areas of growth is crucial to a successful transition into a new career field. It starts with a self-audit of what one can do against the requirements of the target position. This kind of audit will not just show the current skills that one already has, but will also show the areas that need to be developed to match the expectations of a new career line.

A skill gap analysis is an analytical process whereby the skills needed in a desired position are compared with the existing skills and abilities. This type of comparison can help recognize the spheres that should be trained or experienced. Knowing these gaps, people can shape their learning and development activities in order to fill certain shortcomings and, thereby, increase their employability in the new area.

It is also important to identify growth areas. Growth areas are the skills that, though not yet in demand, will prove to be vital as industries change with time. Being ahead of the curve means identifying these new skills and trends early enough so that individuals can place themselves in good positions in the job market. This vision demands life-long learning and active professional development.

People are able to access a wide range of education to fill the skills gaps. These involve taking formal classes, attending classes, or utilizing online learning sites that provide a wide range of subjects. Other informal processes of learning, including mentorship and self-study, can also be influential in acquiring skills. Identifying mentors who have already made other transitions in their careers would be invaluable, and it would offer valuable understanding and advice on how to make a successful transition.

Besides this, professional associations and networks in the industry will also be useful in unlocking resources and knowledge that is not readily available. Even on such networks, you are bound to come across events, seminars, and conferences where you can learn and do some networking with the industry leaders. Such engagements with these communities will not only form part of skills development but will also assist in keeping abreast with industry trends and best practices.

To ensure the continuation of progress in skill development, it is important to set specific learning objectives and monitor progress. Using online tools and templates to chart developmental aims can help to approach skill learning in an organized way. Considering the progress of learning on a regular basis contributes to the revision of the learning strategy. It ensures that the time and effort spent on learning are oriented to career objectives.

Finally, the identification process for skills deficit and developmental areas cannot be confined to the resolution of acute deficiencies. It is concerned with the cultivation of an attitude of constant enhancement and flexibility. Such people can also be relevant and competitive in their fields of choice by investing in lifelong learning and adjusting to change. This active form of personal and professional growth results in improved employment opportunities and leads to personal fulfillment and job satisfaction in life.

Finally, it is important to note that skill gap identification and resolution is an active and dynamic process. It involves self-examination, planning, and an intent to develop. Through a blend of academic learning, mentoring, and individual studies, individuals are able to negotiate career change and reach their career dreams effectively.

Learning Modalities

When it comes to career change, the quest to acquire new knowledge and skills is the cornerstone of success. The variety of modes of learning that are present in the modern world provides one with an abundance of options to personalize their learning process. These modalities go all the way to formal learning and informal, self-administered learning, and each of them possesses its own advantages, which serve different learning orientations and purposes.

Formal education is one such avenue, and it incorporates the usual academic programs like degrees and certifications. Such programs tend to offer a well-organized environment that has a defined curriculum that gives a broad picture of a discipline. It is a particular style that is particularly helpful to individuals who desire to be rooted in a deep understanding of a new discipline, supported by the authority of established institutions. Formal education is organized in such a way that learners can develop a strong base of knowledge, which a network of peers and professionals in the industry can usually complement.

However, in addition to formal education, the introduction of online learning platforms has transformed access to knowledge and made it possible for people to follow their own pace of learning. Coursera, Udemy, and edX are all platforms that provide courses offered by some of the top universities and organizations, and their subjects span a wide range. This is the best mode of study because it is flexible. After all, an individual can learn anywhere and at any time. Choosing individual courses that are more relevant to their interests or their career objectives gives learners the power to shape their own journey through education, and concentrate on the areas that are of greatest interest to their career.

Mentorship and coaching are other invaluable forms of advice and guidance, yet they are personalized. Mentoring work also allows career changers to access the wisdom of professionals (not just knowledge). This is a highly relational kind of learning, which frequently creates long-term professional relationships that go beyond the learning period. Mentorship is especially beneficial when one needs to acquire specific knowledge or wants to learn to make complicated transitions in their career.

Experience and self-study are also important in career development. This mode promotes active exploration among people, as they use books, podcasts, and publications within the industry. A self-study habit promotes a lifelong learning practice, and being an initiator of learning new techniques. In contrast, experiential learning is learning by doing - and this can be in the form of projects, internships, or volunteering. This is not only a practical experience that improves theoretical knowledge, but practical skills are also acquired that are directly applicable in the workplace.

There are also other learning and networking opportunities through professional associations and industry groups. Workshops, seminars, and conferences also provide the people in these communities with a chance to be exposed to the current trends and developments in the industry. These conferences give them an opportunity to share ideas, projects, and professional networks, which can help in advancing their careers.

Simply put, the multiplicity of current learning modalities means that career changers can now afford to customize their scholarly experiences according to their own needs and conditions. Individuals can also prepare themselves with the skills and knowledge required to succeed in new career environments by capitalizing on a combination of formal education, online classes, mentorship, self-study, and professional networking. The broad-based approach not only enhances technical competence but also promotes adaptability, permanence, and a lifelong commitment to personal and professional growth.

Setting Learning Goals

One of the most important points of transitioning to a successful career change is to set learning goals. These objectives act as a roadmap, as they help career changers navigate through the process of learning new skills and knowledge that will enable them to enter the new field. Developing effective learning objectives involves formulating learning objectives that are both effective and aligned with the existing skill set and the needs of the desired career, so that time and effort are directed towards effective outcomes.

Learning goals should be established with a critical self-assessment. This is done by assessing the competences held and recognising deficiencies that must be addressed to suit the requirements of the new career. Such an evaluation must be fair and thorough, considering both hard and soft skills. One should be able to understand the technical capacities that are demanded, as well as the behavioral competencies that are considered important in the new sphere.

After identifying the skill gaps, the next thing to do is to rank the skills that are most important during the transition. Such a prioritization helps in the formulation of specific, measurable, achievable, relevant, and time-bound goals (SMART). The SMART goals are precise and targeted, and it is therefore simple to track progress and to motivate. An example would be a career changer who is moving to the technology sector and has a SMART goal of finishing a code bootcamp within six months, where they can learn the basics of programming.

Besides setting SMART goals, it is also good to develop a learning plan that will outline the tools and tactics that will be used to meet the SMART goals. This action plan may involve taking online classes, participating in seminars, or being mentored by relevant professionals in the industry. Learning plan must be able to integrate a schedule that is both personal and professional, and thus, the learning process will be long-term.

Another important part of having learning goals is to engage in continuous learning. The fast-evolving employment market always needs career changers to be flexible and willing to learn new skills as their careers progress. A culture of lifelong learning can help people remain competitive and ready to embrace opportunities in the future. This encompasses not only formal learning but also informal learning experiences such as networking with other individuals in the industry, webinars, and reading relevant publications.

Seeking feedback and revising goals when necessary is another important component of setting learning goals. It can help you become aware of your progress and of what you have to improve through self-reflection and feedback, particularly that of your mentor or peers. The cyclical process aligns learning objectives with career objectives and industry trends so that the career changer can switch and adjust where necessary.

Finally, milestones and achievements during learning must be celebrated to ensure the process continues. The acknowledgment of any progress, however slight, supports the work and commitment to change the career towards success. These accomplishments help career changers to keep a positive attitude and keep working towards their final career objectives.

To conclude, the process of setting learning goals is dynamic and strategic, and it also requires self-assessment, prioritizing goals, planning, ongoing learning, feedback, and celebrating accomplishments. All these factors enable career changers to successfully negotiate the dynamics of moving into a different profession and have the ability and the confidence to succeed.

Avoiding Repeat Dissatisfaction

The role played by the congruency between personal and professional values in the career change process cannot be underestimated. Periodic self-evaluations are also important milestones in ensuring that the new career venture still matches the values and lifestyle goals. Through conducting periodical audits, one can conclude whether his current job position suits his principles and desired balance in life. This continuous cycle will ensure that the dissatisfaction that could have resulted in the first career change does not repeat.

It is important to identify the initial problems of misalignment. These indicators can include the progressive loss of energy, the feeling of alienation, or the inconsistencies between individual values and the demands of the working environment. The lack of such signals might lead to serious career dissatisfaction, unless addressed accordingly. There is thus a need to learn how to pick up these early warning signs and act proactively to respond to them.

The process of reflection can help in this continual alignment. Regular self-assessment, e.g., after six months of work, can involve evaluating the degree of satisfaction, difficulties, and personal growth in the current job. Such reflections may be prompted or supported by prompts or worksheets aimed at helping gain better insight into career satisfaction. This not only serves to define areas of concern but also to define successes and progress, to help one develop a balanced view of their career path.

Once the dissatisfaction has been determined, one can take several steps to get back on track with his or her career. Some may involve restructuring the existing position into one that is more compatible with an individual's strengths and interests, internal transfers to jobs with higher compatibility, or even pivoting capabilities to find new opportunities in the organization. New projects or initiatives can also be proposed to jump-start interest and bring a sense of purpose and fulfillment.

In addition to a personal change, mentoring can also be a two-way win to strengthen personal development and help others go through a career change process. Individuals can expand their professional circle and their own growth by becoming a mentor or champion to future career changers. Giving advice, anecdotes, and experiences will not only benefit the mentees but also strengthen the knowledge and proficiency of the mentor with regard to his or her own career path.

Being a mentor or a leader in the community can make someone extremely visible and credible in his or her business. Holding local events, organizing questions and answers, or producing content about their career experience are all powerful methods to give back to the community. These activities are not only beneficial to others but also strengthen the role of the mentor as a thought leader and influencer in his or her community.

This reflection and alignment can be additionally improved by using digital tools. Digital tools such as interactive worksheets, milestone monitors, and forums can help provide continuous support and hold the individual accountable. These can serve as resources that guide individuals to ensure that they check back on themselves on a regular basis, discuss with the community, and stay informed of the latest trends and information in the field.

Ultimately, the trick of avoiding dissatisfaction recurrence in a career transition is a reflection/adjustment/community involvement cycle. People can build a satisfying and sustainable career by remaining sensitive to personal values and professional fulfillment, and actively engaging in personal and social development.

Chapter 11: Networking Without Fear

The New Rules of Networking

The old ways of networking have evolved in the new world of professional development, no longer relying on the old dynamics of shallow relationships and the strictly transactional nature of networking. This has introduced a more significant and real opposition to the construction of professional relations when a true focus on real relations and value creation through the creation of mutual values is used instead of exchanging business cards.

This modern network philosophy is based on the belief that the essence of connections lies in generosity and actual interest in others. Rather than taking the attitude of networking as an opportunity to get, the thinking changes to helping. And "what's your story?". This practice creates a space in which relationships are cultivated, based on common ground and cooperative experiences, and on which the opportunities, which are premised on trust and mutual respect, are built.

Networking in this digital age has crossed geographic lines, taking advantage of systems such as LinkedIn, Twitter, and small communities in Slack to build and sustain relationships. These digital tools provide a flexible channel through which members of the profession can facilitate meaningful dialogues, exchange their knowledge, and work together on matters of common interest, regardless of their location on the globe. Thoughtful comments and participation in industry-specific groups can help people create a powerful network that is not limited by geographical boundaries.

Having definite networking goals and purposes has entered the realm of this new paradigm as a fundamental element. Precisely outlining what he/she wants to gain out of networking helps an individual to treat each face with a purpose and focus. It is a tactical measure to ensure that the networking activities are aligned with individual and career objectives and that individuals have the best opportunities to develop significant relationships.

One significant instrument in this new world of networking has been the informational interviews. These casual interviews offer an avenue to gain industry knowledge and company culture, as well as gain trust with professionals in the preferred areas. With the help of step-by-step outreach templates and scripts, people will be capable of making the first step in these conversations and feel confident and ready to face every interaction.

Digital-first strategies also become significant as the development of networking focuses on. Living in an age of remote working and online connectivity is essential, and you need to know how to build and develop relationships online. One can promote his/her online presence and professional development by engaging online communities and sharing useful content, attending online events, or engaging in online conversations.

Finally, new networking rules provide professionals with an incentive to develop relationships that are not only short-term positive but also long-term, sustainable, and rewarding. With the right attitude of collaboration, inquisitiveness, and contribution, one can sail through the challenges of career development with assurance and strength. This transformation of transactional to transformational networking not just enriches professional journeys but also helps to create a more interconnected and supportive professional ecosystem.

Informational Interviews

When it comes to transitioning to a new career, informational interviews also play a key role in collecting information and broadening the professional network. These meetings are typically informal and inquisitive in tone, and they enable career changers to explore the ins and outs of a new industry or position, giving them a plethora of information that is both practical and motivational.

The informational interview is all about providing an unadulterated insight into an occupation or industry. Non-formal job interviews are not about getting a position but are a learning and relationship-building exercise. They also give one a chance to learn about the realities of a job, skills needed, and the challenges that one may be exposed to on a daily basis. This is priceless information because it enables career changers to make informed choices, level out their expectations, and recognize how to develop their skills.

An informational interview involves finding and contacting people who are already in the field that a person wishes to be in. This may be with LinkedIn, professional contacts, or acquaintances. It is essential to create a meaningful and personal message; it must show that you are really interested in the life chosen by the person and that you want to know more about his/her life. Proper outreach will create an opportunity to discuss what would not have been discussed otherwise.

Preparation is important once a meeting is scheduled. One needs to do some research about the industry and the background of the person to prepare some questions. The questions must seek to unearth the complexity of the job, the culture of the company, and the direction of the industry. Asking questions such as What do you like most about your work? Or "What are the essential skills of success? Promote a discussion that is informative and interesting.

Active listening is the most important feature during the interview. By showing real interest and appreciating the time of the interviewee, the interviewer will be able to establish a more transparent and candid conversation. Note-taking is important, and the notes will be useful in subsequent career choices. In addition, a thank-you note as a follow-up to the interview serves as an excellent way to cement the relationship and can result in additional opportunities.

Informational interviews are also used to demonstrate personal abilities and experiences in a rather subtle way. Although the main goal is to learn, it can be useful to share the related experience, build credibility, and create an unforgettable impression. Such a balance of inquiry and the ethos of low-level self-promotion can lead to a lasting professional relationship.

In addition to providing an understanding of the industry, informational interviews can also open up both known and unknown career opportunities. They tend to discover the secret job market, jobs that are not being advertised but instead being filled via referrals and networking. This dimension explains the need to develop a broad and deep network.

To the person changing careers, these interviews are a tactical move in this change. These provide clarity, less uncertainty, and confidence, and help individuals make their career shift with greater confidence. Through these talks, career changers get to understand the possible roles and develop a web of friends who can help them in their career paths.

Finding and Approaching Mentors

When it comes to the transition stage of a new career, finding and building relationships with mentors can become a life-changing experience. The mentor is able to provide guidance, knowledge, and information that are not easily accessible otherwise. When working on a career change, it can be invaluable to find someone who has experienced a successful career change. These mentors not only introduce their knowledge of the new field, but they also understand the problems and opportunities of such a transition.

The search for a mentor should begin by defining what a good mentor is. An appropriate mentor must also possess relevant experience in the field of interest, the desire to help others, and an inclination towards different backgrounds and views. The above attributes guarantee that the mentor will offer customized tips and help to anyone coming out on a new career avenue. Besides, when a mentor has pivoted her or his career, then they can provide a special understanding of the process, as they are the first people to experience the difficulties and successes of the process.

The second step after identifying these qualities is to identify possible mentors. This is done through practical approaches like targeting people in the target industry, firm, or online community. This could be done with LinkedIn. Seeking case studies of career switchers or simply listening to webinars on the industry are good methods to find potential mentors. Such sites and conferences expose us to people who have not only been educated but are also actively involved in their disciplines.

Outreach to potential mentors needs to be respectful and persuasive. The messages should be genuine and show sincerity about admiring the career path of the mentor. Here is an example: a message might begin, I like the way you do it between [old field] and [new field]--may I ask you a few questions about your way? This is respectful and interactive, and it encourages mentors to discuss their experiences without feeling forced.

Once contact is made, it is important to nurture the mentor relationship. This means communicating with the other person on a regular basis, showing appreciation, and making the relationship reciprocal. To maintain the relationship, it may be beneficial to schedule regular check-ins, provide updates, and identify ways to help the mentor in small ways. These are a form of exercising the bond and also show the desire to follow the guidance.

Developing a network of mentors may be included as part of a larger plan to establish a Career Change Brain Trust. This includes creating peer support circles within which individuals may provide peer support, share experiences, accountability, and encouragement. Virtual or face-to-face monthly gatherings can help create a feeling of community and purpose in people going through similar transitions.

Finally, identifying and recruiting mentors becomes a key element in learning how to change careers. Career changers can receive invaluable support and insight by identifying the appropriate mentors, approaching them with honesty, and developing the relationships. These relationships can open the door to an easier changeover and offer guidance and inspiration to them as they start their new careers.

Building a Career Change Brain Trust

Think about getting a group of fellow travelers together who are all in unique transitions and have their own unique perspectives, experiences, and thoughts. This is what a career change brain trust is all about--a select assembly of colleagues who provide accountability, support, and new perspectives as you start the process of redefining your professional life. The power in such a group lies in its ability to provide a safe environment where the challenges and the successes can be shared, and where a positive atmosphere can be created, and beneficial feedback and learning can thrive.

Brain trust is based on the assumption that it might be highly effective to support the process of career change through collaboration. By placing yourself in the circles of those also in the transition process, you form a network that not only empathizes with the complexities of undertaking such a transition but also helps in the development of each member. It is this mutual support chain that becomes a point of inspiration and creativity, and all kinds of experiences are tapped into in order to solve a problem and celebrate the achievement.

Identifying potential members with similar goals and values in their objectives is the first step in forming or joining a career change brain trust. This may include connecting with alum clubs, attending industry-related conferences, or even engaging in discussions on professional sites such as LinkedIn. The trick is to locate those who take their career transitions seriously and are willing to share their experiences and stories.

After the group has been established, it is important to establish a routine of meetings. These meetings may be held online or in real life, depending on the location and desires of the members. The meetings must be arranged but loose so as to accommodate premeditated dialogues and spontaneous intercourse. One such session might be a round table where everyone presents an ongoing challenge and a recent triumph to establish a problem-solving and supportive group atmosphere.

Besides holding regular meetings, the brain trust may also be enriched with rotating hot seat sessions. This is characterized by a group of people giving their attention to one of its members, with a specific issue or decision the member is struggling with. The other members of the group then provide advice, feedback, and possible solutions based on their own experiences and knowledge. This type of format can not only provide the individual in the hot seat with valuable information, but also build a critical and sympathetic mindset within the group.

An environment of trust and confidentiality is an important part of a successful brain trust. The members must not be afraid of being judged or having their privacy violated when they share their opinions and experiences. It is this trust that helps the group to become a true source of support and innovation.

In addition, it can be highly helpful to utilize the feedback of peers. It could be refining a resume, learning how to interview, creating a personal brand, or any other aspect of the process. Still, the critical feedback and the different viewpoints provided by the group can result in some major gains and discoveries.

Finally, career change brain trust is not a support group, but a dynamic and evolving network that can effectively respond to the emerging needs of its members. The ethic of collaboration and human growth is a solid foundation on which individuals can develop a system of managing the complexity of the career change practice with enthusiasm and in a good mood.

Chapter 12: Managing Your Digital Footprint

Cleaning Up and Amplifying Online Presence

The online world has turned the process of controlling what is posted online into personal branding, and each element matters. The need to have a clean and professional online presence has become especially essential as people seek to negotiate the challenges of a career transition. Hiring managers and recruiters are becoming more dependent on online profiles when evaluating prospective employees, and it is therefore essential that career changers showcase an online profile that reflects their new professional goals.

The initial part of this changing process is to carry out a thorough online audit. This includes a careful screening of their online profile, beginning with a basic search of their name in well-known search engines. The aim is to find and remove old or unnecessary material that is no longer beneficial to the career goals of the individual. All old blog posts, tweets, or any other public content that may not represent the preferred professional image should be examined and updated or removed.

Another important consideration is platform consistency. An integrated digital identity is the key to making sure that all professional profiles (LinkedIn, personal websites, or any other social media platforms) tell the same story. This is updating the bios, making sure that professional titles and descriptions are consistent across platforms, and aligning them to the new career path. By so doing, career changers will succeed in presenting their new professional persona to prospective employers.

It is also important to amplify the positive digital signals. This is possible through contributions to relevant discussions in the online communities and active participation in the relevant online communities that are aligned with the new career path. Becoming a member of industry-specific groups on networking platforms such as LinkedIn, Slack, or Facebook can contribute to building a network and increasing visibility in the new field. Posting knowledge leadership content, like articles or blog posts on the new industry, can make a person appear as an experienced and dedicated professional in their field of choice.

In addition, privacy and reputation are two important aspects to manage in order to remain professional online. It should be noted that it is necessary to establish the limits on what is posted publicly and to modify the privacy settings. It is also important to deal with any negative or controversial material. Be it a reply to old negative news or a controversial post, handling the situation tactfully and professionally can help reduce the damage that can be done to the reputation.

In general, the cleanup and amplification of online presence is not a one-time activity but a continuous process. It needs updates and interactions with routine so that the digital footprint does not become obsolete and is fixed on the previous career progress of the individual. Career changers can do a lot to improve their probabilities of success in their new careers by strategically managing their presence online.

Leveraging Social Proof

Social proof is effective because it builds trust and credibility, which may be necessary when individuals are experimenting with new careers. In a world where cynicism can be more dominant sometimes than talent, the use of testimonials, endorsements, and references is a strategy worth its weight in gold. As a career changer, it may not be easy to prove competence in a new area. Testimonials and third-party recommendations are also great ways of closing this gap by giving external credibility to the skills and potential of an individual.

The only way to successfully utilize social proof is by first knowing its importance. Social proof is a form of psychological and social behavior in which individuals imitate the behavior of others in an effort to replicate the appropriate behavior in a particular circumstance. When it comes to career transitions, it serves to dispel the natural cynicism that usually comes with a move to a new industry. When your potential employer notices that other people have already recommended your skills, it gives them the confidence that you are good and capable.

Career changers need to request strategically to be recommended in ways that highlight their flexibility, learning agility, and transferability. It can be invaluable to request former coworkers, bosses, or clients to leave testimonials that directly speak to these attributes. It can be beneficial to provide a clear context and specific examples of skills that match the new career direction and prompt those writing the testimonials to concentrate on the related strengths. One would be an email template that implies I would be delighted if you would mention my cross-functional team leadership skill, which I believe I can bring into the project management skills area that I require in my new domain.

It is also important to include such endorsements in branding documents. Testimonials can easily be included in LinkedIn profiles, resumes, and personal websites as quotes to support your story. Having an apposite pull-quote on your personal site, or a featured comment in a LinkedIn profile, can alert recruiters and hiring managers to your skills and give a great demonstration of your ability.

Along with conventional written suggestions, career changers can become more credible and creative. An example of such a dynamic and engaging method of presenting the endorsement is video testimonials. A few short videos of your mentors or co-workers talking about your best side can be a great addition to your online portfolio. Likewise, a managed reference highlights document can be a one-page referral sheet that hiring managers can use during the hiring process.

In addition, a group of champions and mentors within the new industry can be an ongoing source of support and additional layers of social cues. These people may serve as champions, and they can provide personal recommendations and introductions that open gateways to new opportunities. These connections can be achieved through networking practices and joining industry-specific associations that can help create presence and reputation in the new area.

Overall, the use of social proof is a matter of strategically displaying recommendations and testimonials that demonstrate applicable skills and flexibility. It must be carefully incorporated into personal branding activities and an initiative to create networks that support. In this way, social proof will help career changers successfully manage the process of transitioning into their new careers, surmounting the effects of skepticism, and earn the trust that leads to success.

Creating a Digital Portfolio

Creating a digital portfolio is a necessary process for any career changer. A portfolio created in the digital era is an efficient way to show your skills, experiences, and accomplishments appealingly. A digital portfolio can be more dynamic than a traditional resume, and it gives a better understanding of what you are capable of doing to potential employers, a feature that a traditional resume lacks.

A digital portfolio must also be carefully designed to reflect the personal brand and the particular career path you are following. The first thing to do is to determine the core competencies and experience that best apply to your target industry. This is through a keen choice of projects, case studies, and successes that reflect your capability to produce results in various setups. Everything in your portfolio must have a story and should show not only what you accomplished but also the outcome of your work.

Images are very important in creating a difference in your portfolio. Use quality images, videos, and infographics to depict your projects and accomplishments. These elements turn your portfolio into an interesting piece of content, but they also demonstrate your ability to explain complicated information clearly and creatively. Where feasible, provide links to ongoing projects, publications, or any other resources online to which you have contributed, as a concrete demonstration of your competence and experience.

Your online portfolio must have an intuitive and user-friendly design. Break down your content into precise headings and categories to make sure a potential employer can find the information they want as quickly as possible. An effective design, paired with a consistent branding composition, logos, color schemes, and typography, will support your personal brand and create a memorable impression.

Along with displaying your previous achievements, your portfolio must also demonstrate how you continue to devote yourself to professional growth. Add a section that contains your ongoing activities, studies, and what you plan to achieve. This shows not just your knowledge but also your initiative toward development and adjustment in a very dynamic employment environment.

The online portfolio is not just a compilation of your samples of work; it is your professional identity in the form of a portfolio. So, you should update your portfolio regularly, add new projects, and delete the old ones. Not only does this make your portfolio interesting, but it also demonstrates that you are interested in what you are doing.

On top of that, testimonials or personal recommendations can also provide much value to your portfolio. It can be written recommendations, video testimonials, or reviews on platforms such as LinkedIn. Positive evidence of your social qualities and benefits in prior jobs can significantly increase the trustworthiness of your resume.

Last but not least, make a digital portfolio available on different devices and platforms. An adaptable design will make your portfolio not only look good, but also work on a desktop, tablet, and smartphone. Also, think about the security and privacy of your portfolio by utilising quality hosting solutions and paying attention to what information you decide to make public.

Simply put, a digital portfolio that is developed properly is a strategic asset throughout the career change process. Not only does it display your skills and accomplishments, but it also acts as a marker of your professionalism, creativity, and willingness to face new challenges.

Protecting Your Online Reputation

In the era of the internet, when one single click, post, and share can radically change the course of one's career, shaping an online identity has become as important as maintaining a professional resume. With the continued use of the internet by more employers and recruiters to screen their potential employees, it cannot be overemphasized that individuals be careful of their digital footprint, keeping it clean and professional. This is not just with the deletion of undesirable images or controversial online postings, but also with a conscious effort to create an online persona that aligns with your career interests.

Having a comprehensive review of your current online presence is the beginning of securing your online reputation. Begin with a research of your name on different search engines and know what potential employers can learn about you. This practice can assist you in determining any old or outdated information that may not be applicable to your present working status. It is necessary to look through the previous posts of the blog, Twitter, or comments that could be unprofessional or controversial. This material can be erased or revised to prevent potential confusion or bias.

As soon as the cleanup is complete, the amplification of positive digital signals should be considered. It includes keeping your online profiles on sites such as LinkedIn as up to date as possible and making them relevant to your current career goals. Writing a strong LinkedIn profile, such as, is not about writing down a job history. It must have a carefully considered overview of your abilities, successes, and visions that appeal to the target audience. Industry keywords should be used to maximize the search engine visibility of your profile, and thus recruiters can more readily locate you.

In addition to LinkedIn, participate in professional forums and post to online organizations in the area of interest. Posting insightful articles, attending webinars, or writing thought-leadership content can go a long way towards enhancing your professional image. These activities not only show that you are informed, but also show that you want to contribute to your field.

Another important part of reputation management is privacy settings on social media platforms. Change these settings so you can decide who views your posts and information. It is important to exercise caution regarding the nature of information you post publicly, as even the posts that seem to be quite innocent to share can be misunderstood. Moreover, it is prudent to revisit and reset these settings after some time, as platforms keep changing their privacy policies.

Dealing with bad online content is also a component of controlling your online reputation. Where you have undesirable material that you are unable to delete, could you do what you can to mitigate it? This may include how to address negative remarks professionally or giving context to explain any misconceptions. In other instances, they may need professional assistance in dealing with more severe reputation problems.

Lastly, building a good network of professional relationships can also be used as a social verification. The endorsement and recommendation of reputable colleagues and leaders within the industry can go a long way to promote your credibility. Ask your peers to write recommendations about you, highlighting your strengths and contributions. Such recommendations can sometimes outshine the lesser bad content and make you appear like a trusted, worthy professional.

Nowadays, in the dynamic digital world, it is crucial to be proactive and intentional in your online activity. Not only can you safeguard your reputation by seizing control of your online story, but you can also access new career opportunities. This is a proactive method of marketing yourself online so that when your name is keyed into the search engine, the recruiters get a refined, professional, and persuasive profile of who you are and what you have to offer.

Chapter 13: Staying the Course: Sustaining Momentum

Tracking Your Journey

Each action performed during the career change process requires careful consideration and careful planning, just like a carpenter carefully carving a work of art. Everyone has a distinct starting point in the complex dance of career evolution, and each must follow a journey as intimate to him or her as it is transformative.

Please think of how it would feel to wake up to a day when the possibilities of your professional future are limitless. The atmosphere is new, and it is filled with the promise of new life. This day is the starting point of a conscious effort to redefine work as it means to you. The purpose behind a career change is often the deepest want of one to find the occupation that corresponds with their personal values, the pursuit of meaning and satisfaction that cannot be found within the standard occupational limits.

In this transformative process, the act of reflection serves as a compass. Self-assessment is important to know what drives you and what drives you to achieve. What drives you? What are the intrinsic values that you cannot compromise on? These are not rhetorical questions, but the basis of a valid and viable career change plan. In answering these reflective questions, you start to draw a map of your ideal career world.

The idea of establishing milestones becomes inevitable as you go over this route. The signs of development, the signs of personal development, which serve as the motivators and the inspirers, are they. Every inch forward is a credit to endurance and flexibility, which are essential in traversing the sometimes stormy landscape of transitioning careers. These benchmarks offer the framework that is necessary to make abstract objectives concrete and become actual accomplishments.

The career change process also requires a willingness to learn and adjust constantly. The business world is ever-changing, and one has to be ready to adopt fresh new knowledge and skills in order to stay relevant. This can include formal training, course training, or even experience training in new positions. The lifelong learning commitment will not only improve professional capabilities but also create a growth and innovation mindset.

Community and support are priceless values in this growing narrative. Networking with mentors and peers is very valuable and motivating. These relationships provide a supportive space in which ideas may be shared, difficulties may be overcome together, and victories may be shared. The experience is enhanced by the experiences that other people have undergone during their journey.

Finally, the idea of tracking career change is a far more personal and, at the same time, global journey. It is a process of self-reflection, education, and development guided by the desire to follow the profession that will help to connect with all one's most cherished values and dreams. With every single step, the way becomes increasingly obvious, the goal of a career of purpose and fulfilment grows nearer, and it starts to become apparent not as a far-flung dream, but as something that can be achieved.

Celebrating Milestones

Every move forward in the complex dance of career transformation is a testament to perseverance and outlook. A consciousness of such measures not only warms the drive but also refreezes advancement to become a professional reinvention. And a congratulations celebration is not a license to spend but an essential practice that will continue energy and investment in change.

The key to this practice is the appreciation of major accomplishments and minor wins. The smaller wins are easy to forget about, but they are the blockbusters, which create the foundation of bigger success. These micro-wins help an individual have a growth mentality that is receptive to improvement and instill a culture where motivation thrives. This level of acknowledgment serves as a great antidote to the natural instances of self-doubt and exhaustion that come with any serious change in life.

Think of the feeling of accomplishment after struggling through a difficult certification that seemed impossible before. When this is celebrated, it is a light in the darkness as it throws light on the way ahead. It can be a pat on the back with an understanding friend or a reward all to yourself, a day off to rest; these celebrations are the checkpoints that are important milestones on the journey.

Celebration is a very personal act and must appeal to what is joyful and fulfilling. Others may feel better being alone, thinking about their accomplishments over a quiet dinner, and others may feel more comfortable with the companionship of those who share their experience and understand the ins and outs of their path. The trick here is to make celebrations suitably reflective of what adds value to the spirit and strengthens the promise to the course taken.

Besides, milestones should not only be celebrated to look back and feel proud but also to prepare to achieve more in the future. It is a time to take a break and rebalance. When one goes through what went right and what can be made better, there is always an invaluable amount of information that leads to the next action. This type of self-reflective practice makes the practice of celebration strategic as an instrument of continuous improvement.

This can be further improved by including milestones in a systematic plan. An effective milestone map that plans short-term, mid-term, and long-term goals offers a clear way in which progress can be monitored. These maps not only explain the journey, but also bring into reality and action the abstract idea of career change. The achievement of each milestone is evidence of fortitude and flexibility by dividing the bigger objective into smaller, easy-to-accomplish tasks.

These milestones can have more power when they are shared with a community. When people recognize the accomplishments of others, it becomes a new aspect of meaning. One of the means that a person may speak to others about his or her progress and understand how to become one of them, and a cause is the mentorship group or peer support. These communities act as a sounding board and a source of inspiration and therefore encourage their members to go beyond perceived boundaries.

Finally, celebrating milestones means giving importance to the path, just like the end. It is a practice that helps generate strength, inspiration, and a success narrative that propels one. Each large or even small milestone is an episode in the story of transformation, a lesson of what it takes to reinvent oneself as a professional. By doing so, one is not only taking a step in the right direction, but one is also perpetuating a cycle of growth and success that defines a successful career change.

Building Resilience

During a career transition, the skill of adapting and recovering after failure is important. Being resilient is not merely about being able to withstand tough times but also about flourishing in those times and using them as a chance to develop. Resilience is a crucial quality in a world where there are few linear career paths to follow, but one needs to be able to pivot successfully.

The initial phase of resiliency-building is the acceptance of the fact that failures are inseparable from any career change. This knowledge can be used to redefine these disappointments as learning rather than failures. This way of thinking prompts a person to perceive challenges as information, which gives feedback instead of final destinations. Thinking about failures as a lesson, which can be constantly improved, allows one to become more resilient in his or her approach.

Another important aspect of resilience is developing a growth mindset. Psychologist Carol Dweck popularized this philosophy, and its key point is that abilities and intelligence can be trained over time and effort. When it comes to career changers, a growth mindset equates to taking challenges on board, persevering through challenges, and viewing effort as a means of mastery. The objective of practical exercises, like journaling and reflection, is to enable people to solidify such an attitude by emphasizing progress over perfection.

The development of a support network is also a form of building resilience. Being around individuals who are supportive and who will give constructive feedback will provide the emotional and psychological support required when changing careers. Meeting with mentors, joining professional organizations, or attending peer support groups may provide new insights and perspectives and can strengthen determination. These networks may also serve as sounding boards for ideas and offer support in times of uncertainty.

In addition, celebrating small victories also helps people become stronger. Micro-wins should be identified and rewarded, which will build confidence and motivation and provide physical evidence of progress. This habit helps to keep the momentum and gives a psychological buffer against failures. These accomplishments, however small they are, should be monitored, and they all lead to the bigger picture.

The other dimension of resilience is coping with stress and emotional health. Changing careers tends to be a frustrating experience, and it is important to have a plan to deal with the frustration. A positive attitude of calm and control can be held through mindfulness exercises, including meditation or deep breathing exercises. Exercise, sleep, and proper eating are also important in maintaining overall health, which directly affects the ability to stay resilient.

As a rule, the process of resilience building is a complicated process that intersects change of mind, support systems, and self-care. Another characteristic of a resilient person is the ability to change strategies and plans in response to new information or unexpected events. This fluidity also makes a person flexible and receptive to new developments, even when the original plans fail to work out as intended.

Lastly, it is no simple task since resilience building alters attitude, social support, and self-care. It involves learning through failures, embracing minor achievements, coping with stress, and being open to change. To persons who are going through the turbulence of a career transition, resilience might be the difference between mere survival and success in new career environments.

Thriving in Your New Career

It can be difficult to adjust to a new career because it can be like entering a new territory, where the well-known signs of success and accomplishment are absent. However, in this ambiguity, there is the germ of personal and professional development. The first few days of any new job are full of a sense of excitement and a sense of fear. The trick to success is to accept this duality and leverage it to a system that is, at the same time, resilient and adaptive.

The initial weeks matter a lot and determine how the rest will be. It is the time of being submerged in the culture and rhythm of the new place. This silent yet powerful introduction is observed, as well as the unspoken rules, knowing people who are on your side, etc. Every engagement, be it a quick hallway talk or a business gathering, provides a peek into the organizational canvas. Here, listening is a priceless instrument--not only listening to what is said, but also to the tones and shades that are so easy to miss.

Another pillar of success in a new career is the establishment of relationships. Active contact with colleagues and stakeholders should be sought. Arranging a first meeting may be a good strategy to loosen the ice and build rapport.

Such interactions do not only entail chit-chatting but also avenues of getting to know what it is like to be on the other end of the debate and to hear what is expected of them. They offer an opportunity to identify with the larger interests of the team and organization, and they form a sense of belonging and a mission.

When the first dust settles, attention should be paid to value delivery. Wins early in the season can easily increase confidence and credibility. It is also helpful to find easy wins, work, or projects that a person can put the already acquired strengths into action to generate momentum. Even the smallest of these successes can act as a building block to even greater successes. They provide an opportunity to demonstrate personal skills and reaffirm one's position in the team as well.

Learning and adapting are an essential part of survival in a new profession. This is when it is possible to detect the presence of skill gaps and make active efforts to combat them. The idea is to remain relevant and competitive, whether it is formal training, mentorship, or self-directed study. The attitude of lifelong learning not only leads to the improvement of the range of skills but also resilience in dealing with challenges.

Positive reinforcement is a great developmental tool. Taking an initiative to get feedback and embrace constructive criticism can speed up the learning curve. One should think of feedback as a gift--a chance to get better and better. Incorporating constructive feedback contributes to aligning individual work with what the new environment demands and requires.

Lastly, work/life balance is critical in achieving success in the long term. Setting boundaries, self-care, and healthy work-life balance are essential in avoiding burnout. Prospering in a new profession is not only about career performance but also about growing and developing oneself.

Successful survival in a new career is, in a way, a process of exploration and development. It means finding a way to survive in difficulties, seizing the chance, and developing constantly. This is because, by being in relationships, pursuing constant improvement, and leading an even-handed life, one can not just survive but thrive in the new position.

Chapter 14: Giving Back: Mentorship and Community Leadership

Becoming a Mentor

The career transition journey to being a mentor is a complex process that supports both the mentor and the mentee. It begins with understanding how significant the power of sharing experiences and knowledge can be to other people who are going through a similar experience. Mentorship is not only about leading others but also reflecting on how and where one has gone in their career, learns what to avoid, and applying that wisdom to guide others in their own transitions.

Self-reflection is the initial part of becoming a mentor. This includes making a reflection on the career path that a person has walked, the lessons that have been learned, and the obstacles that have been overcome. In this way, the potential mentors will have a better insight into the specific knowledge they will be able to contribute. Such self-understanding not only enhances the confidence of the mentor but also makes sure that the mentor bases their advice on real-life experience and compassion.

After the self-reflection process, the second step is to find platforms to share such knowledge with other people. This may be formal mentorship programmes in the industry networks or informal mentoring of colleagues or new entrants into the industry. Giving career change workshops, writing articles/posts on blogs about oneself, and attending online forums are all good methods of reaching a larger audience and establishing oneself as a resource of knowledge.

Listening is an important part of being a good mentor. The key is to know the goals, challenges, and concerns of the mentee. Active listening helps a mentor provide advice that best fits the unique requirements of the person and builds a positive and effective relationship. This individualized practice will not only improve the experience of the mentee, but the mentor will also gain insights into emerging worldviews and issues in the changing career environment.

Furthermore, mentorship is a two-way relationship. Although a mentor guides, he/she also learns new lessons and is inspired by his/her mentees. It is this sharing of ideas that can lead to new modes of thinking and problem-solving, and this keeps mentors active and in a continuous state of learning. Moreover, the process of mentoring other people can also strengthen the skills and knowledge of the mentor themselves, because most of the time during the process of teaching, one is enhancing his/her knowledge of a certain topic.

Mentors also need to work on equipping mentees with critical skills and confidence. This may involve giving feedback on personal branding, contributing to the creation of networking strategies, or assisting in finding and seeking skill-building opportunities. Mentors enable mentees to have a solid base for a successful career change by empowering them in these areas.

Finally, expectations and limits need to be set in order to be a mentor. You also need to be clear about the kind of relationship that is going to exist between the mentor and the mentee and how it will be mutually advantageous. This makes the relationship mutually beneficial and also sustainable in the long run. Maintaining a good mentoring relationship requires information with regard to availability, desirable channels of communication, and the area of support that will be offered.

Finally, the mentoring process is professional and personal. It involves a commitment to knowledge sharing, an openness to listening and learning, and the capacity to motivate others. Adopting a mentor role not only helps the other person to succeed but also allows the individual to feel even more accomplished in their career.

Impact of Community Leadership

Community leadership is a core part of a career change journey and has many benefits that are not limited to personal success. It can be described as a driver of personal development, a feeling of belonging, and a favourable environment, in which experiences and general wisdom are exchanged and thrive. Community leadership is, at its most fundamental, about moving past personal aspirations to become a source of light to others, leading them through whatever changes they may be undergoing in their careers.

The nature of community leadership is that it helps to create networks of support and encouragement. When people assume the leadership role in their communities, they provide a platform upon which knowledge and experience can be shared freely. This will not only help demystify the career change process but also help facilitate mutual learning. Community leaders also make the career-change process more accessible and less intimidating by telling success and failure stories that can help others understand how to pursue a new career.

In addition, community leadership leads to increased visibility and credibility. When they popularize the cause of career change, they will automatically attract attention to themselves and their professionalism. With this visibility, new opportunities can be opened, not only to themselves but also to the people they inspire. Exposure is an individual activity that leaders can establish in their respective fields through active engagement in community-based events, including meetups or webinars that may result in professional development and networks.

Another way in which community leadership influences is the culture of mentorship that it promotes. Leaders are often mentors, having to provide advice and care to individuals who are transitioning through their own career changes. Such mentorship may be formal, in the form of organized programs and initiatives, or informal, in the form of informal discussions and guidance. Mentoring others not only helps leaders to reinforce their own learning and development, but it also helps them to leave a legacy of support that makes the entire community stronger.

Community leaders facilitate the creation of inclusive environments that celebrate diversity of thought and experience. They develop an interest in a wide spectrum of backgrounds, and also ensure that the community has the perks of a mosaic of diverse perspectives. It is an incredibly important diversity in the context of innovation and creativity, because more ideas and solutions can be generated.

Moreover, community leadership is something that gives a sense of responsibility and mission. The desire to leave a significant mark is often a powerful motivator that leads leaders to have greater goals and expectations both towards themselves and the communities they serve. This purpose is potentially so empowering that it gives the leaders the strength to get through these difficulties and disappointments.

In summary, community leadership plays an enormous role in the career change arena. It is a facilitating and inspiring atmosphere in which people can learn, develop, and flourish. Community leaders can be extremely important in defining the future of career transitions through building relationships, increasing visibility, and supporting mentorships. The value of their contributions is that they not only benefit those who make individual career changes, but they also enhance the greater community, producing a ripple effect of positivity that spreads far beyond their own circle.

Leveraging Digital Companion Tools

The digital age relies on the use of technology in personal and professional development. The accompanying digital companion portal to the book is a very resourceful tool that can be employed to augment the experience of the career changer with a myriad of interactive tools and services. This portal can be viewed as a central source of downloadable worksheets and milestone trackers and a vast repository of resources designed to help people effectively navigate their career transitions.

The portal has been carefully structured with templates and video tutorials that deliver step-by-step instructions on different issues regarding career change. These tools are designed to ensure that users not only plan their career moves but also do them with accuracy. They might include templates like personal branding rules or a career change plan, and video lessons might include information on how to succeed in job interviews or networking.

One key characteristic of the portal is that it is accountable and aimed at growth using interactive tools. Users should be able to use those digital tools in their daily life; therefore, they should cultivate a disciplined attitude towards career advancement. Progress check-in reminders are one such tool that automates reminders to keep users on track and ensure that they are achieving their personal and professional milestones.

The other pillar of the portal is community engagement. It also gives users the opportunity to join online community forums, where they can communicate with other users, exchange experiences, and receive knowledge from other users who are on the same path. These forums allow answering questions within the community Q&A sections and joining virtual accountability groups, which can be helpful in keeping the motivation up and getting encouragement throughout the process of changing careers.

In addition, the portal has emphasized the need to remain current with new, real-time information and professional knowledge. Weekly webinars, real-time podcasts, and updates on new jobs in the market, which the portal offers, do this. Their value to users cannot be overstated in keeping them abreast with current trends and opportunities in the fields of their interest. They can be launched as monthly professional webinars or podcast episodes, during which the most recent information and plans are presented by the heads of the industry, and live data laboratories, during which up-to-date information on employment patterns is shown.

When individuals are empowered with the experience and resources required to make informed choices and take constructive action in their professional change, through the mobilization of these digital tools, the portal is a source of information as well as a trigger of personal and professional growth. Through these resources, the users will be able to advance their competencies and networks and ultimately pursue their career dreams with a sense of enhanced confidence and competency.

Conclusion and Call to Action

A career change process is not an end in itself, but a process of becoming a different person, which is a transformation of one job into another, but also a gesture of endurance and flexibility. Upon reaching the end of this life-changing guide, we are supposed to look back at the profound journey that the readers have undergone during their process of dealing with the uncertainties and challenges that accompany the change of career.

In the process, people have been prepared with the information and resources needed to help them overcome the initial fears and doubts that usually haunt career changers. The shift of the state of uncertainty into the state of clarity and confidence requires the adoption of an attitude to accept change and perceive challenges as sources of learning. The book has been a roadmap: It has taken readers through the most important steps to achieve success in life, starting with self-awareness and evaluation of one's own values and strengths, passing by opening new opportunities and creating a strong personal brand.

Readers have been taught to tap into their individual talent and experiences and turn them into resources that fit into their new career directions. Through their strategic networking and use of new technologies, they have created narratives that appeal to potential employers and demonstrated their flexibility and willingness to work in new areas. The specified strategies are written in order to solve the mysteries of career transition, and the real activities are made to get material results.

The journey does not end here. The process of career change is a long-term process that requires constant reflection, learning, and change. The lessons learned and the competences acquired during the course of this book are not only the tools to help the reader during one transition but the lifelong resources that will benefit readers in their future lives. Adopting a lifestyle of continuous learning and an open-mindedness towards new opportunities can keep people on their feet and ready to face anything the future may bring.

The spirit of exploration and the boldness to take a step forward are what readers should bring to the very beginning of their new life. Be it reaching out to a new acquaintance, applying to a position that appears unattainable, or even mentoring those who are on their own paths, the call to action is obvious: keep practicing what I have learned, reach out to the community, and help people through their transitions.

The web-based companion materials and community forums that this book provides are invaluable and provide this continuity and interconnectiveness. With these communities, the reader is able to share his or her stories, seek advice, and give advice, which also helps in supporting the idea that he or she is not alone on this path. The feeling of belonging and collective cause present in these networks can be an overwhelming drive, and can help to maintain the momentum and encourage further expansion.

And this chapter, as we come to a close, should not be the end but a stepping-stone towards a future of potential and promise. The instruments, techniques, and support mechanisms discussed herein are geared towards helping the reader create not only a successful but also a very satisfying career. It means that with a sense of direction, with a desire and a belief in continuous personal and professional growth, the future is clear and promising. You can take on this new phase with confidence and curiosity, knowing that the process of learning the art of career change will be a lifelong process that is full of discovery and accomplishment.

EPILOGUE

As you close the pages of this book, reflect on the journey you've embarked upon one filled with introspection, transformation, and empowerment. This book has been your guide, offering a roadmap through the complexities of career change, with each chapter serving as a stepping stone toward a future crafted by your own hands.

You have navigated through the initial fog of uncertainty, where dreams and doubts entwined, and emerged with a clearer vision of your path. By identifying your core values and strengths, you've laid the foundation for a career that aligns with your true self. The exercises and reflections have not just been tasks, but opportunities for profound self-discovery, revealing the unique blend of skills and passions that define you.

At the heart of your transformation lies the art of storytelling. You've learned to articulate your narrative, weaving past experiences into a compelling story that resonates with new opportunities. This narrative is not just a tool for others to understand you; it is a testament to your resilience and adaptability.

The strategies for networking and job searching have armed you with the skills to navigate the modern job market with confidence. You have built a brand that reflects your aspirations and engaged with a community of like-minded individuals, ensuring that you are never alone on this path.

As you step into the next phase of your career, remember that change is not a destination, but a continuous process. Keep the momentum alive by staying curious, embracing lifelong learning, and remaining open to new possibilities. The digital companion portal remains at your disposal, a treasure trove of resources to support your ongoing growth.

Celebrate your achievements, no matter how small, and use them as fuel to propel you forward. Please share your experiences, mentor others, and become a beacon of inspiration for those who, like you, seek fulfillment and purpose in their professional lives.

In closing, know that you possess the tools, insight, and courage to design a career and life that you love. This book has merely been the catalyst; the true journey unfolds with each decision you make and each step you take towards a future that is truly yours.

www.ingramcontent.com/pod-product-compliance
Lightning Source LLC
Chambersburg PA
CBHW060324050426
42449CB00011B/2636